THE REAGAN YEARS

Doonesbury books by G.B. Trudeau

·G.B.TRUDEAU·
DOONESBURY DOSSIER

THE REAGAN YEARS

INTRODUCTION BY GLORIA STEINEM

HOLT, RINEHART AND WINSTON
NEW YORK

Library of Congress Catalog Card Number: 84-80587
ISBN Hardbound: 0-03-061729-4
ISBN Paperback: 0-03-000072-6

First Edition

Designer: Paul Gamarello/Eyetooth Design
Printed in the United States of America

The cartoons in this book have appeared in newspapers
in the United States and abroad under the auspices of
Universal Press Syndicate.

10 9 8 7 6 5 4 3 2 1

ISBN 0-03-061729-4 HARDBOUND
ISBN 0-03-000072-6 PAPERBACK

For Biff and Rickie

· Four Good Reasons for Reading This Book ·
(ANY ONE OF WHICH SHOULD BE ENOUGH)

By way of research for writing this, I read the introductions—written by Garry Wills and William F. Buckley, Jr., respectively—for the first and second big *Doonesbury* anthologies.

The Wills essay was a well-researched report on the early characters and characteristics of *Doonesbury*'s world. Its premise was that this new-style comic strip's success and trademark came from carrying a hip sportscasting style into social comment on every area of American life. "Almost every one of us so-called adult male Americans," Wills explained in his very first sentence, "is a jock manqué."

The Buckley essay was a personal account of his surprise at liking something as frivolous as a comic strip. Buckley explained that he first heard of Garry Trudeau while looking at "the names of people fetching honorary degrees" at Yale, and finally read a collection of *Doonesbury* strips only after being asked to write an introduction. "There are the anticlimaxes," Buckley notes in his role of critic, "but the reader forgives them indulgently; he is well enough nourished, all the more so since there is all that wonderful assonant humor and derision in mid-panel; indeed, not infrequently the true climaxes come in the penultimate panel, and the rest is lagniappe."

Well, I am neither a jock manqué nor a Yale man. I am not crazy about phrases like "not infrequently," people who say "fetching" (unless they are British), and commentary phrased like Buckley's "the longueurs are sometimes almost teasingly didactic." Therefore you might wonder why three such disparate people should be writing praisefully about one and the same creation.

This proves the first virtue of Trudeau's work: it brings very diverse people together. Because *Doonesbury*'s world stretches from campus to Washington, from American bedrooms and football fields to the battlefields of the Mideast and American blunders in Southeast Asia, it includes more varieties of characters than any other comic strip, not to mention more than most movies or novels. No wonder the readers who find themselves connected by their mutual liking for *Doonesbury* are very diverse indeed. What else could be shared by arch-conservative William Buckley, who does not even think female Americans should be included equally in the Constitution, as well as by me and other feminists; or, for that matter, by Garry Trudeau himself, who also campaigned long and hard for the Equal Rights Amendment and for feminist politicians? Not much.

Such bringing together could not be accomplished by papering over or downplaying real differences of opinion, and Trudeau would never attempt that. On the contrary, he uses the differences themselves as the source of much of the humor in *Doonesbury*. Furthermore, no character, whatever her or his beliefs, gets past the Trudeau pen without the little inconsistencies that make us human and vulnerable and that allow even our deepest enemies to become mysteriously understandable. Right smack in the middle of a real conflict, passionate belief, or confrontation, there arrives that moment of uncertainty or endearing personal *schreck*—often in, as Buckley would say, "the penultimate panel"—that allows us to smile and empathize with each other.

The second reason to read this book has to do with change. If this doesn't sound too pushy, it even has to do with redemption.

Unlike most of his comic colleagues who refuse to let their characters age, much less change their minds or personal styles, Trudeau's people grow, take on new ideas, change their jobs and even their personal worlds. For instance: Joanie Caucus, a burgeoning feminist, managed to live more or less peacefully in a campus commune with a jock who chose only the most obedient of girlfriends, young women whom Joanie tried valiantly to subvert. The jock took his turn at communal cooking, even if he did so with his football helmet on. When he had to go off to Vietnam, we realized just how vulnerable, and how valuable, a mindless jock could be. The same Joanie became campaign manager for Ginny Slade, a black woman with the courage to run for Congress, and with a boyfriend named Clyde who didn't think she should be a candidate at all; yet Clyde campaigns for her in white racist neighborhoods and finally admits that he is proud of her. Lacey Davenport, a patrician Congresswoman fairly distant from brand-new-lawyer Joanie's homemaker background and liberal/radical beliefs, nonetheless hires her as a Congressional aide out of respect for Joanie's past behavior in the opposition camp. Rick Redfern, an egocentric Washington investigative reporter, falls in love with Joanie and (almost) allows her to save him from becoming a gossip columnist for *People* magazine. The list of changes and surprising personal journeys goes on and on. Even the worst terrorist, the most pure of female Maoists, the most vacuous of television commentators, or the least competent of Presidents may turn out to have a saving grace and a change of heart.

This gives us faith. If the *Doonesbury* characters we love and identify with can change and be redeemed, surely we, the readers, can change and be redeemed too.

Of course, none of this would be possible if Trudeau did not *like* his characters; or, to say the same thing in a more realistic way, if he were not capable of seeing at least one touching quality in people he doesn't like very much, and at least one inconsistency in people he likes and admires.

This talent for empathy, the third reason for reading this book, also separates Trudeau from the Jules Feiffer–ish tradition that, given the political content they both share, would otherwise be an obvious parallel. Feiffer's world yields a kind of amusement and instruction that is similar to *Doonesbury*, but his people make us feel a little superior; a dead giveaway of the fact that their creator probably feels a little superior to them, too.

According to H.W. Fowler's classic definitions of the purposes of various forms of humorous comment, this means that Feiffer's function is more that of satire and sarcasm, whose objects are "amendment" or "inflicting pain," whose province is "morals and manners" or "faults and foibles," and whose audience is the "self-satisfied" or "the bystander." The Trudeau function, on the other hand, is more what Fowler defines as humor and wit, whose objects are "discovery" and "throwing light," whose province is "human nature" or "words and ideas," and whose audience is "the sympathetic" and "intelligent."

Furthermore, satire and sarcasm are defined as having "accentuation" or "inversion" as their method, while humor and wit are defined as employing "observation" or "surprise," and Trudeau's powers of observation are nearly unlimited. Who else could show us a rock superstar who is surprisingly, touchingly knocked out by his wife's pregnancy and the birth of their first child? Or the upper-class, bird-watching husband of Lacey Davenport, who survives the obscenity of being a Congressional spouse in Washington, and who for thirty-five years has been in his wife's words "the most interesting man at any party."

Those subleties are worthy of the best novel; yet Trudeau packs them all into a few lines of dialogue and into even fewer drawings. *Doonesbury* shows us a life that is all the clearer for being compressed. It brings us an imaginary garden that unites a whole world of disparate toads.

By allowing us to smile *with* characters rather than *at* them, Trudeau also allows us to admit just how like one or more of these characters we may be.

That's the fourth and best reason for reading this book. Where else can you smile while growing and learning?

DID ZONKER GET OFF ALL RIGHT?

OH, YES, AND HE WAS A WONDER TO BEHOLD!

HE'S LAID DOWN ONE OF THE BEST BASES I'VE EVER SEEN. HE'LL KNOCK 'EM DEAD AT THE OPENING CEREMONIES!

I DIDN'T KNOW THERE WERE OPENING CEREMONIES!

OH, ABSOLUTELY. THE GERALD R. FORD SUMMER BIATHLON IS NOTHING IF NOT POMP AND CEREMONY!

MR. PRESIDENT! WE WHO ARE ABOUT TO FRY SALUTE YOU!

GERALD R SUMME BIATHLO

..AND THE FINAL SCORE SHALL BE DETERMINED BY FACTORING YOUR GOLF SCORES WITH THE METERED DIFFERENTIAL BETWEEN YOUR STARTING AND FINISHING TANS!

POINTS WILL BE DEDUCTED FOR UNEVENNESS OF TANNING, OF COURSE, AND PEELERS, OF COURSE, WILL BE DISQUALIFIED.

IT NOW GIVES ME GREAT PLEASURE TO OFFICIALLY OPEN THE 1980 GERALD R. FORD SUMMER BIATHLON!

LADIES AND GENTLEMEN, START YOUR TANS!

GO! YEA!! GO!

..AND REMEMBER TO KEEP YOUR CHIN UP. WE DON'T WANT ANY UNSIGHTLY WHITE SPOTS!

DON'T SWEAT IT, BERNIE, I'LL BE FINE. IT'S THE GOLF THAT'S GOT ME WORRIED.

FORGET THE GOLF! YOU'VE GOT TO CONCENTRATE ON A STRONG START! REMEMBER, KID, THE TWENTY-MINUTE FREESTYLE IS YOUR BEST EVENT!

SO GET OUT THERE AND DEVELOP YOUR KIND OF TAN! MAKE THEM COME TO YOU!

NO WAY, MAN. LAST TIME I TRIED THAT, A GUY WOUND UP IN THE HOSPITAL WITH THIRD-DEGREE BURNS!

ZONKER, TANNING'S A ROUGH SPORT! PEOPLE GET HURT!

SOME OF THEM ARE JUST KIDS, BERNIE! I WON'T HAVE ANY PART OF IT!

GERALD R. FORD SUMMER BIATHLO

GO! DO IT!

GO FOR IT!

GERALD R. FORD SUMMER BIATH

LADIES AND GENTLEMEN! THERE ARE THREE MINUTES REMAINING IN THE FIRST HEAT!

GERALD R. FORD SUMMER BIATH

GO! GO!

CLAP! CLAP! CLAP!

POUR IT ON!

THINK HE'LL MAKE HIS MOVE SOON?

YES! THERE! HE'S WIPING OFF HIS SUNSCREEN!

TERRIFIC START, ZONK! YOU WIPED EVERYONE OFF THE DECK! PICKED YOUR FINAL TAN YET?

WELL, I'D STILL LIKE TO USE "FREEWAY BOLD" SONNY BONO'S OLD TAN. THINK I CAN MAKE IT?

WELL, THE COURSE LOOKS PRETTY TOUGH—NOT MUCH SHADE. BUT WITH THE LEAD YOU NOW ENJOY, YOU COULD JUST LAY BACK TODAY AND DEVELOP A PRIMING COAT..

THEN, ON DAY TWO, IF YOU GO ALL OUT, YOU COULD PROBABLY ACHIEVE FULL COLOR BALANCE BY THE 16TH HOLE, LEAVING A TWO-HOLE MARGIN FOR TOUCH-UP WORK.

I'D GO FOR IT. PIECE OF CAKE.

I KNOW. I JUST HOPE I DON'T EMBARRASS SONNY.

NOT A BAD LIE. WITH A GOOD CHIP, I SHOULD HIT THE APPROACH CLOSE TO THE GREEN.

THE SUN'S HIGH, BUT I THINK WE'LL BE GETTING A WISP OF CIRRUS CLOUD COVER. STILL, COULD BE ROUGH ON MY SHOULDERS.

HMM..

WHAT DO YOU THINK?

LET'S TRY A SEVEN IRON AND A #2 SUNSCREEN.

ZONKER, WITH PROFESSIONAL TANNING BECOMING SO LUCRATIVE AND PRESTIGIOUS, HOW COME YOU DON'T FIND RINGERS COMPETING—YOU KNOW, BLACKS AND HISPANICS?

BECAUSE TANNING IS JUDGED BY DIFFERENTIAL. PEOPLE WITH DARK SKIN DON'T GET MUCH DARKER IN THE SUN.

THEN WOULDN'T YOU SAY THAT THE SPORT OF TANNING DISCRIMINATES AGAINST BLACKS?

NO MORE THAN BASKETBALL DISCRIMINATES AGAINST SHORT PEOPLE.

BUT IN COMPETITIVE TANNING, A PERSON IS ACTUALLY JUDGED BY THE COLOR OF HIS SKIN, RIGHT?

WELL, SURE, BUT..

I JUST THINK WE'RE ON THIN ICE HERE.

GO! GO!

WOW.. LOOK AT THAT GUY ON THE 16TH!

HUH?

YEA!! GO FOR IT!

WHAT A GLOW. JUST LOOK AT HIM SOAKING UP THOSE RAYS!

HE MUST BE WORKING WITHOUT A SCREEN.

GASP!

UH-OH.. LOOKS LIKE HE OVERDID IT..

SUNSTROKE! SERVES HIM RIGHT.

MEDIC!

POOR SAP..

THE KID WAS HOTDOGGING. HE KNEW THE RISKS.

THANK YOU, MIKE. I CERTAINLY APPRECIATE THAT FINE INTRODUCTION.

MY FRIENDS, AS YOU KNOW, IT HAS BEEN OUR GREAT PRIVILEGE THIS YEAR TO CONDUCT A POLITICAL CAMPAIGN OF IDEAS..

WHEN FACED WITH THE DISMAL CHOICE PROVIDED BY THE TWO-PARTY SYSTEM, WE HAVE DARED TO ASK OURSELVES, WHY NOT A GENUINE ALTERNATIVE? WHY NOT JOHN ANDERSON?

BECAUSE HE DOESN'T STAND A CHANCE!

HUSH, DICK! IT WAS A RHETORICAL QUESTION!

J.J., I WANT YOU TO MEET MIKE DOONESBURY. HE'S AN OLD FRIEND FROM WALDEN, AND I'VE ASKED HIM TO STAY THE NIGHT.

HI, J.J.

HI.

WELL, GUESS I'LL TURN IN. J.J. WILL SHOW YOU YOUR ROOM, MIKE. DON'T YOU KIDS STAY UP TOO LATE.

THANKS FOR EVERYTHING, JOANIE.

SETUP CITY.

HEY, I WANTED TO STAY AT A MOTEL, BUT SHE WOULDN'T LET ME.

SO. MIND IF I HAVE A SEAT, J.J.?

SUIT YOURSELF.

THANKS.

SO WHAT ARE YOU WATCHING?

TELEVISION.

HEY, THAT'S GREAT. LOOKS LIKE A PRETTY GOOD CHANNEL, TOO.

YOU KNOW, J.J., I'M REALLY PLEASED TO MEET YOU FINALLY. I'VE ALWAYS WONDERED WHAT YOU WERE LIKE..

I'VE NEVER FORGOTTEN HOW MUCH YOUR MOTHER USED TO TALK ABOUT YOU THAT SUMMER SHE HITCHED A RIDE WITH ME FROM BOULDER..

WAIT A MINUTE! YOU MEAN, YOU WERE THE GUY WHO GAVE MOM A LIFT ON HIS MOTORCYCLE?

WELL, ME AND MY FRIEND MARK. IT'S HIS MOTORCYCLE, BUT I USE IT A LOT.

OH, WOW! YOU GUYS WEAR LEATHERS?

LIVE IN THEM. THIS IS JUST BORROWED.

WELL, THAT'S OUR SHOW TONIGHT ON "THAT'S AMAZING, AMERICA!" WE HOPE YOU HAVE BEEN AS AMAZED AS WE HAVE!

BEFORE WE GO, THOUGH, OUR PRODUCERS WOULD LIKE TO THANK ALL THOSE INCREDIBLE FOLKS WHO HUMILIATED, DEBASED OR DISFIGURED THEMSELVES JUST FOR THE CHANCE TO APPEAR ON TELEVISION!

WITHOUT YOU, THIS SHOW WOULD BE NOTHING! WE LOVE YOU ALL, AND WE WILL BE SENDING EACH OF YOU A "THAT'S AMAZING, AMERICA!" T-SHIRT!

NEXT WEEK: A 93-YEAR-OLD HOOKER SPEAKS HER MIND! UNTIL THEN, BE AMAZING, AMERICA!

YEAA!!

CLAP! CLAP! CLAP! CLAP!

WHATCHA WORKING ON, MIKE?

MY NOTES.

YOUR NOTES. FOR WHAT?

A PHONE CALL. I MET THIS GIRL IN WASHINGTON LAST MONTH AND I WANT TO ASK HER UP FOR A WEEKEND.

YOU NEED NOTES TO TALK TO HER ON THE PHONE?

KEEPS ME FROM CLUTCHING. I NEED SOME KIND OF NET. TELL ME IF YOU THINK THE TONE OF MY OPENING IS RIGHT..

"HELLO, J.J.? IT'S MIKE. NO, MIKE. MIKE DOONESBURY. WITH GLASSES, REMEMBER?"

IT'S A BIT DEFENSIVE, BUT BETTER SAFE THAN SORRY, YOU KNOW?

MIKE, DO YOU ALWAYS USE NOTES WHEN YOU CALL A GIRL ON THE PHONE?

DON'T YOU?

WELL, NO, NOT ORDINARILY..

YOU SHOULD TRY IT. I FIND I HAVE A LOT MORE CONFIDENCE IF I'VE WORKED OUT WHAT I'M GOING TO SAY IN ADVANCE.

ALSO, IT FREES ME TO THINK OF SPONTANEOUS STUFF THAT I CAN THEN PEPPER THROUGH THE CONVERSATION.

LIKE WHAT?

OH, BASEBALL SCORES, QUIPS, STUFF FROM THE NEWS — YOU KNOW, LIKE JOHNNY CARSON DOES.

MAY I SPEAK TO J.J. CAUCUS, PLEASE?

SPEAKING.

"J.J.? HI, THIS IS MIKE."

WHO?

UH..MIKE. MIKE DOONESBURY. OH, NEVER MIND. YOU WOULDN'T REMEMBER. GOOD-BY..

NO, NO, MIKE, DON'T HANG UP! I WAS JUST KIDDING! LET'S TRY IT AGAIN, OKAY?

"J.J.? HI, THIS IS MIKE."

ECSTASY!

..AND THEN AT 3:00, WE TAKE IN A MOVIE, AND AT 4:45, WE GO OVER TO RUDY'S FOR A DRINK!

MY! IT SOUNDS LIKE YOU'VE GOT A WHOLE SCHEDULE WORKED OUT.

WELL, ACTUALLY, I DID PREPARE A SMALL LIST OF THINGS I THOUGHT MIGHT BE FUN TO DO..

THERE'S SOME FREE TIME ON THERE, I HOPE.

YEAH, BUT I'M AFRAID WE'VE ALREADY USED UP ALMOST TEN MINUTES OF IT.

MIKE, WHAT IF WE JUST HAP-PENED TO MIS-PLACE THAT OL' SCHEDULE OF YOURS?!

NO PROBLEM - I'VE GOT THE MASTER ON FILE. YOU ALMOST THROUGH WITH YOUR HAMBURGER?

UH..YEAH. JUST GIVE ME A MINUTE.

G B Trudeau

HI, KIDS!

OH, HI, MARK!

J.J., I'D LIKE YOU TO MEET MARK SLACKMEYER. HE'S ONE OF MY ROOM-MATES!

HI, MARK. NICE TO MEET YOU.

NICE TO MEET YOU, J.J.!

SO HOW'S THE DATE GOING?

NOT SO GOOD. WE'RE TEN MINUTES BEHIND SCHEDULE.

HOLD ON! I'M ALMOST THROUGH!

G B Trudeau

BOY, WHAT A SCARY MOVIE!

YEAH, IT'S PRETTY SCARY, ALL RIGHT..

UNFORTUNATELY, I DON'T THINK WE'VE GOT TIME TO STAY UNTIL THE END..

WHAT? ARE YOU NUTS? LEAVE BE-FORE WE FIND OUT WHO KILLED HER?

I ALREADY KNOW. IT WAS THE PSYCHIATRIST.

MICHAEL!

I'M SORRY, J.J. IT'S JUST WE'VE ONLY GOT AN HOUR TO GET DRUNK BEFORE THE CONCERT.

..AND THE BATH-ROOM IS DOWN THE HALL TO THE LEFT. YOU'RE MAD AT ME, AREN'T YOU, J.J.?

NO, I'M NOT MAD AT YOU, MIKE. JUST EXASPERATED!

I JUST DON'T KNOW WHY EVERY MINUTE HAD TO BE SO CHOCKED WITH ACTIV-ITIES! WHY COULDN'T WE JUST DO WHAT WE FELT LIKE AT THE MOMENT?

I'M SORRY, J.J.. I GUESS I DID SORT OF OVERPLAN. I WON'T PUT YOU THROUGH THIS AGAIN, I PROMISE..

TOMORROW'S SCHEDULE IS A LOT MORE FLEXIBLE..

FORGET IT, BUB! HAND IT OVER!

G B Trudeau

THE HUMAN BRAIN. ONE OF LIFE'S GREATEST MIRACLES. STAGING AREA FOR THE 1,000,000 CHEMICAL REACTIONS A MINUTE THAT SHAPE HUMAN RESPONSES, RESPONSES WHICH IN SOME CASES AFFECT THE OUTCOME OF HISTORY ITSELF.

GOOD EVENING. FOR FOUR YEARS NOW, WE HAVE HAD THE CHANCE TO WATCH JIMMY CARTER'S MIND AT WORK. BUT WHAT OF RONALD REAGAN'S MIND? WHAT DO WE KNOW ABOUT IT? DOES SCIENCE REALLY KNOW WHAT MAKES HIM TICK?

I'M ROLAND HEDLEY. JOIN ME TONIGHT AS ABC UP-CLOSE NEWS TAKES A JOURNEY INTO THE UNKNOWN — A FANTASTIC VOYAGE THROUGH.. THE BRAIN OF RONALD REAGAN!

"REAGAN'S BRAIN", BROUGHT TO YOU BY ANACIN..

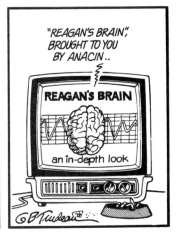

REAGAN'S BRAIN

an in-depth look

HI! WELCOME TO THE MYSTERIOUS WORLD OF RONALD REAGAN'S BRAIN! HOME OF NEARLY 30 BILLION NEURONS, OR "MARBLES," AS THEY ARE KNOWN TO THE LAYMAN!

WHAT WONDERS AWAIT US! THE FORNIX—REAGAN'S MEMORY VAULT, STOREHOUSE OF IMAGES OF AN IDYLLIC AMERICA, WITH 5¢ COKES, BURMA SHAVE SIGNS, AND HARDWORKING WHITE PEOPLE!

THE HYPOTHALAMUS, THE DEEP, DARK COILS OF HUMAN AGGRESSION, SOURCE OF REAGAN'S IMPULSES TO SEND U.S. FORCES TO ANGOLA, IRAN, KOREA, CYPRUS, CUBA, LEBANON AND COUNTLESS OTHER HOT SPOTS!

SO FASTEN YOUR SEAT BELTS! IT'S A TOPSY-TURVY FUNHOUSE OF A TRIP, BUT YOU WON'T BE SORRY! NOW THIS.

FIRST STOP, THE LEFT HEMISPHERE OF REAGAN'S CEREBRUM. TRADITIONALLY, THIS IS THE HOME OF LOGIC, ANALYSIS AND CRITICAL THINKING. LET'S TAKE A CLOSER LOOK..

AS YOU CAN SEE, MANY NERVES IN THIS PART OF THE BRAIN ARE FRAYED. THE RIGORS OF THE CAMPAIGN TRAIL, PARTICULARLY THE LACK OF SLEEP, HAVE TAKEN THEIR TOLL.

STUDIES HAVE SHOWN THAT SUBJECTS NOT ALLOWED TO SLEEP AND DREAM BECOME HIGHLY DISTURBED. THE BRAIN NEEDS TO DREAM; IF DEPRIVED AT NIGHT, IT COMPENSATES BY HALLUCINATING DURING THE DAY.

SEEN IN THIS LIGHT, MR. REAGAN'S ABILITY TO RECONCILE HUGE TAX CUTS WITH MASSIVE MILITARY SPENDING MUST BE VIEWED WITH SOME SYMPATHY.

REAGAN'S CEREBELLUM. HERE WE ENCOUNTER A MAZE OF NEURONS AND THEIR DENDRITIC SPINES, FROM WHOSE TIPS INFORMATION IS TRANSMITTED BY ELECTRICAL IMPULSES.

INTELLIGENCE IS THOUGHT TO BE RELATED TO THE COMPLEXITY OF THESE CONNECTIONS. UNHAPPILY, THE BRAIN STOPS GROWING AT AGE 20, AND THEREAFTER, NEURONS DIE OFF BY THE MILLIONS EVERY YEAR.

WHAT THIS MEANS IS THAT THE BRAIN OF RONALD REAGAN HAS BEEN SHRINKING EVER SINCE 1931, WHEREAS JIMMY CARTER'S BRAIN CELLS HAVE ONLY BEEN DYING SINCE 1944.

TO THE TRAINED SCIENTIST, THIS REPRESENTS A CLEAR CHOICE. BACK AFTER THIS.

WE'RE UP NEAR THE VISUAL CORTEX NOW, THAT PART OF THE BRAIN RESPONSIBLE FOR PROCESSING STIMULI RECEIVED FROM GOVERNOR REAGAN'S EYES..

UNHAPPILY, A SEVERE PERCEPTUAL DISORDER WITHIN THE CORTEX ITSELF HAS PLAGUED THE CANDIDATE'S VISION FOR YEARS..

INSTEAD OF LOOKING FORWARD THROUGH CLEAR EYES, REAGAN IS ONLY ABLE TO SEE BACKWARDS THROUGH A ROSE-COLORED MIST.

TRAGICALLY, HIS CONDITION IS THOUGHT TO BE INOPERABLE.

OUR TOUR ENDS IN THE PRECONSCIOUSNESS, THE MIND'S GREAT STAGING AREA. IT IS HERE THAT REAGAN'S SUBCONSCIOUS THOUGHTS LIE POISED FOR ADMITTANCE TO FULL CONSCIOUSNESS, WHERE THEY CAN THEN BE ANALYZED AND EDITED.

IN RECENT YEARS, HOWEVER, CAMPAIGN PRESSURES HAVE FORCED REAGAN TO SAVE TIME BY CIRCUMVENTING THIS LAST CRITICAL STAGE OF THE INTELLECTUAL PROCESS.

AS A CONSEQUENCE, MANY OF REAGAN'S IDEAS ON SUBJECTS RANGING FROM TREE POLLUTION TO THE KU KLUX KLAN FIND FULL VOCAL EXPRESSION THE INSTANT THEY OCCUR TO HIM.

OUR POLITICAL FOLKLORE IS THE RICHER FOR IT. I'M ROLAND HEDLEY.

..AND NOW IT'S TIME FOR THE UBBY "COPING CORNER"! WITH US TODAY IS OUR OLD FRIEND, DR. DAN ASHER, AUTHOR OF "MELLOW-SPEAK." I'LL LET HIM TELL YOU WHAT HIS NEW OPUS IS ABOUT. DAN?

THANKS, MARK. MY NEW BOOK'S CALLED "THE MELLOW MORTGAGE." IT'S ALL ABOUT REAL ESTATE, HOW IT CAN CHANGE YOUR LIFE AND MAKE YOU FEEL GOOD ABOUT YOURSELF.

MY BOOK HELPS YOU CHOOSE THE REAL ESTATE LIFE-STYLE THAT'S JUST RIGHT FOR YOU, WHETHER IT'S LOTS OR CO-OPS. I SHOW THAT REAL ESTATE IS ACCESSIBLE TO EVERYONE FROM DEVELOPERS TO STRUGGLING NEWLYWEDS! EVEN THE POOR ARE GETTING INTO THE ACT!

THEY ARE?

WELL, THEY CALL IT "TURF," BUT IT'S THE SAME PRIDE OF OWNERSHIP.

SO YOUR THESIS IN "THE MELLOW MORTGAGE" IS THAT REAL ESTATE CAN BE A WHOLE NEW LIFE-STYLE, IS THAT RIGHT, DR. DAN?

FOR MILLIONS OF UPSCALE AMERICANS, IT ALREADY IS, MARK.

ACTUALLY, IT'S A VERY HEALTHY DEVELOPMENT. PEOPLE NO LONGER JUDGE YOU BY WHAT YOU DO. ALL THAT REALLY MATTERS TODAY IS WHAT YOU PAID FOR YOUR HOUSE AND WHAT IT'S WORTH NOW.

IT'S REALLY QUITE A PHENOMENON. AT DINNER PARTIES ALL AROUND THE COUNTRY, STUDIES SHOW THAT THE PREFERRED SOCIAL LUBRICANT THESE DAYS IS NO LONGER BOOZE OR GRASS — IT'S REAL ESTATE!

DOESN'T THAT GET A LITTLE EXPENSIVE?

FOR SURE. THE MARKET FOR GOOD CONDO IS VERY TIGHT.

OKAY, LET'S GET DOWN TO CASES, DR. DAN. WHAT EXACTLY IS A "MELLOW MORTGAGE"? / A MELLOW MORTGAGE IS A SWEET DEAL, MARK..

THAT MEANS A LONG-TERM AGREEMENT WITH A LOW INTEREST RATE AND A SMALL DOWN PAYMENT. IT'S NOT EASY GETTING THESE TERMS, BUT ONCE YOU DO, YOU'RE ON YOUR WAY!

IN MY BOOK, I SHARE MY SECRETS, THE AMAZING TECHNIQUES WHICH CAN PARLAY A MERE $1000 INVESTMENT INTO A SPRAWLING, MULTIMILLION-DOLLAR EMPIRE IN A MATTER OF DAYS!

AND ALL YOU WANT IS $12.95? THAT HARDLY SEEMS FAIR. / IT'S AN INCREDIBLE OFFER, ISN'T IT?

DR. DAN, I WONDER IF YOU COULD EXPLAIN TO OUR LISTENERS WHAT "GENTRIFICATION" MEANS.. / FOR SURE. IT WORKS LIKE THIS: A DEVELOPER BUYS A DILAPIDATED HOUSE IN A DEPRESSED NEIGHBORHOOD..

HE FIXES IT UP AND RESELLS IT TO A YOUNG, MIDDLE-CLASS COUPLE. THIS ENCOURAGES OTHER "GENTRY" TO BUY INTO THE NEIGHBORHOOD, AND BEFORE LONG, A FANTASTIC REAL ESTATE MARKET BOOMS WHERE NONE EXISTED BEFORE! /

AND WHAT HAPPENS TO THE LOW-INCOME TENANTS WHO ARE DISPLACED? DOES ANYONE CARE? / SURE, WE DO. THESE PEOPLE ARE VERY IMPORTANT TO THE WHOLE PROCESS!

THEY ARE? / OF COURSE. THEY MOVE ON TO DEVALUE OTHER PROPERTIES. WITHOUT THEM, THE WHOLE SYSTEM FALLS APART.

DR. DAN, LET ME SEE IF I'VE GOT THIS STRAIGHT. WHAT YOU'RE SAYING IS THAT THE BEST REAL ESTATE INVESTMENTS ARE IN DECAYING NEIGHBORHOODS. / THAT'S RIGHT..

OF COURSE, SOME NEIGHBORHOODS PROVE VERY RESILIENT, SO IT'S OFTEN NECESSARY TO STIMULATE THE AREA'S DECLINE IN ORDER TO BRING DOWN LOCAL PROPERTY VALUES.

HOW DO YOU DO THAT? / NOTHING HEAVY-HANDED. WE MIGHT, FOR INSTANCE, DISTRIBUTE SPRAY PAINT AND CROW BARS TO THE LOCAL KIDS.

YOU GET THEM TO VANDALIZE THEIR OWN HOMES? / WELL, WITHIN LIMITS. WE ASK THEM NOT TO TOUCH THE COPPER PLUMBING.

WHO WAS THAT ON THE PHONE, HONEY? / IT WAS SUZY FROM DOWNSTAIRS. SHE'S BRINGING UP A TELEGRAM FOR ME!

A TELEGRAM? FROM WHOM? / MY GUESS IS IT'S FROM PEKING. THE GANG OF FOUR TRIAL IS ABOUT TO START, AND I'M SURE TO BE CALLED AS A KEY WITNESS.

WHY YOU, HONEY? / WELL, I USED TO BE MAO'S PERSONAL TRANSLATOR. AFTER HIS STROKE, I WAS THE ONLY PERSON IN CHINA WHO COULD UNDERSTAND HIM.

WOW.. SO DID HE REALLY ORDER THE CULTURAL REVOLUTION? / WELL, I THOUGHT SO, BUT I MAY HAVE GOTTEN IT WRONG.

MISS HUAN? I'M COMRADE ZHAO, FROM THE PROSECUTOR'S OFFICE. I'M GOING TO BE BRIEFING YOU ON YOUR TESTIMONY FOR THE TRIAL.

NICE TO MEET YOU, COMRADE. HOW'S THE TRIAL PROGRESSING?

SO FAR, VERY WELL.

THE STATE HAS CLEARLY ESTABLISHED THAT THE GANG OF FOUR IS GUILTY OF GENOCIDE IN THE DEATHS OF 34,375 INNOCENT PEOPLE. THE DEFENSE IS CLAIMING MANSLAUGHTER.

MAN-SLAUGHTER?

THEY SAY IT WAS 34,375 UNRELATED ACTS OF PASSION.

ARE ALL FOUR MEMBERS OF THE GANG BEING TRIED TOGETHER, COMRADE?

YES. ACTUALLY, THERE ARE TEN DEFENDANTS.

THE OTHERS ARE FROM THE CLIQUE OF SIX, A BAND OF REACTIONARY TRAITORS WHO PLOTTED TO ASSASSINATE THE CHAIRMAN IN 1971.

IT'S BEEN QUITE A YEAR FOR OUR NEW LEGAL SYSTEM. ALREADY THIS YEAR, WE'VE PROSECUTED THE MOB OF EIGHT, THE COW-DUNG SIX, THE NEST OF THREE, AND THE FOUR VERMIN.

YOU NAIL THEM ALL?

ALMOST. THE FOUR VERMIN SKIPPED BAIL.

SO HOW'S THE NEW CRIMINAL CODE BEEN WORKING OUT, COMRADE?

WELL, IT'S TAKEN SOME GETTING USED TO..

THE NEW ARTICLES PROVIDE FOR THE PRINCIPLE OF PUBLIC TRIAL AND THE RIGHT TO HIRE COUNSEL. THEY ALSO REQUIRE LIMITED DETENTION AND THE USE OF WARRANTS.

ALL THESE NEW RIGHTS HAVE CREATED CONSIDERABLE CONFUSION. FOR INSTANCE, JUST RECENTLY, "THE STATE VS. THE FIVE COCKROACHES" WAS THROWN OUT ON A TECHNICALITY.

NO KIDDING? WHAT SORT OF TECHNICALITY?

SCHEDULING ERROR. TURNED OUT THEY'D ALREADY BEEN EXECUTED.

COMRADE, ABOUT YOUR TESTIMONY. I DON'T HAVE TO TELL YOU HOW IMPORTANT IT IS THAT THE NAME OF THE GREAT HELMSMAN NOT BE DRAGGED THROUGH THE MUD..

AS HIS INTERPRETER, YOU WERE IN A UNIQUE POSITION TO KNOW IF THE CHAIRMAN REALLY ORDERED THE MURDEROUS EXCESSES OF THE CULTURAL REVOLUTION, AS HIS WIFE CONTENDS.

UH-HUH. WELL, YOU KNOW, COMRADE, THE CULTURAL REVOLUTION WAS SOMETHING OF AN OBSESSION WITH MAO..

YOU MEAN, WITH THE GANG OF FOUR.

RIGHT. DID I SAY MAO? I MEANT THE GANG OF FOUR.

I KNOW YOU DID. THAT'S WHY WE'RE HAVING THIS LITTLE CHAT.

WELL, I THINK THAT ABOUT COVERS IT, COMRADE. WE LOOK FORWARD TO YOUR TESTIMONY IN COURT TOMORROW.

THE GANG OF FOUR HAS COMMITTED TOWERING, MONSTROUS CRIMES. THE BLOOD OF THE CULTURAL REVOLUTION WILL BE ON THEIR HEADS FOREVER.

COMRADE, BETWEEN YOU AND ME, THE GANG OBVIOUSLY HAD A LITTLE HELP. WON'T YOU HAVE TO TRY THOUSANDS OF OTHERS, TOO?

"A SERPENT MAY BE A HUNDRED FEET LONG, YET TO KILL IT, ONLY THE HEAD MUST BE CUT OFF."

NICE. THAT BY MAO?

NO, SOME FACTORY WORKER. WE HAD A CONTEST.

WILL THERE BE MANY PEOPLE AT THE TRIAL, COMRADE?

YES, NEARLY 800 SPECTATORS, IN ADDITION TO THE 35 JUDGES.

35? WHY SO MANY?

AS A SAFEGUARD. WE WANT TO MAKE SURE THERE AREN'T ANY PROCEDURAL MISTAKES..

REMEMBER, MISS HUAN, WE HAVEN'T HAD A REAL LEGAL SYSTEM FOR 30 YEARS. THE WHOLE WORLD WILL BE WATCHING. THE TRIAL OF THE GANG OF FOUR MUST BE JUST AND SWIFT.

THEN WHY THE FOUR-YEAR DELAY?

WE HAD TO GET ALL THE JUDGES THROUGH LAW SCHOOL.

ISN'T HONEY GOING TO BE JOINING US TONIGHT, J.J.?

OH, DIDN'T I TELL YOU? SHE'S BACK IN PEKING.

REALLY? YOU MEAN FOR THE HOLIDAYS?

NO, FOR THE GANG OF FOUR TRIAL..

PRETTY AMAZING, HUH? IT TURNS OUT THAT MY ROOMMATE IS THE GOVERNMENT'S STAR WITNESS IN THE CASE AGAINST MADAME MAO!

THAT'S HER! THAT'S THE MAGGOT!

YOU'RE QUITE SURE, COMRADE?

MISS HUAN, AS MAO'S PERSONAL INTERPRETER, YOU WERE PRESENT DURING HIS WIFE'S SYSTEMATIC PERSECUTION OF ARTISTS AND INTELLECTUALS DURING THE CULTURAL REVOLUTION, WERE YOU NOT?

YES, THAT'S RIGHT.

I WONDER IF YOU COULD TELL THE COURT HOW MANY FATAL PERSECUTIONS YOU PERSONALLY WITNESSED, MISS HUAN.

WELL, LET'S SEE. THERE MUST HAVE BEEN AT LEAST 50, 60, SOMEWHERE IN THAT NEIGHBORHOOD.

THINK HARDER, MISS HUAN. WASN'T IT CLOSER TO 34,000?

WHY..YES! I REMEMBER NOW! THANK YOU, COMRADE.

NOT AT ALL. I COULD SEE YOU WERE BLOCKING.

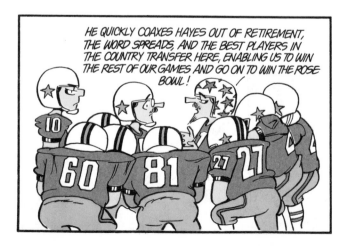

..AND THEN JIANG QING CONFESSED TO YOU HER PLANS FOR THE TOTAL DEVASTATION OF ARTISTIC AND INTELLECTUAL LIFE IN CHINA, DID SHE NOT, MISS HUAN?

YES, OF COURSE, I DIDN'T BELIEVE HER.

OF COURSE NOT. IT WAS TOO MONSTROUS. BUT TELL US WHAT HAPPENED THAT FATEFUL MORNING WHEN THE CULTURAL REVOLUTION ACTUALLY BEGAN.

WELL, I KNEW SOMETHING WAS IN THE AIR, THAT SOME INSIDIOUS FORCE WAS POISED TO DESTROY OUR CULTURE..

HOW DID YOU KNOW THAT, MISS HUAN? WHAT SIGNS WERE THERE?

WELL, TO BEGIN WITH, MY POTTERY CLASS HAD BEEN CANCELLED..

SO THAT TIPPED YOU OFF RIGHT AWAY?

NOW, THEN, MISS HUAN, EARLY IN YOUR TESTIMONY, YOU CALLED MY CLIENT, JIANG QING, A "TREACHEROUS CUR," ISN'T THAT RIGHT?

YES, SIR, THAT'S RIGHT.

AND YET LATER, YOU CHARACTERIZED HER AS A "LOATHSOME COCKROACH," CORRECT?

UH..YES, I GUESS I DID..

WELL, WHICH IS IT, MISS HUAN, A CUR OR A COCKROACH? SHE CAN'T BE BOTH! WOULDN'T YOU SAY THAT'S A RATHER GLARING CONFLICT IN YOUR TESTIMONY?

UM.. WELL, NO, BECAUSE SOMETIMES SHE..

NO FURTHER QUESTIONS, YOUR HONOR.

COMRADE HUAN?

YES?

I HAD THE HONOR OF WATCHING YOUR TESTIMONY THIS WEEK. I WAS WONDERING IF I COULD HAVE YOUR AUTOGRAPH..

MY AUTOGRAPH? UH..SURE!

I CAN'T THANK YOU ENOUGH. ALL OF US WERE SO IMPRESSED BY YOUR BRAVE CONDEMNATION OF THE HIGH-RANKING EVILDOERS.

WHY, THANK YOU.

WAS THIS YOUR FIRST PURGE?

NO, NO, I'VE SEEN 'EM COME AND GO.

MY, MY, WE CERTAINLY ARE COMING UP IN THE WORLD, AREN'T WE?

HOW'S THAT?

"YOU ARE CORDIALLY INVITED TO THE THIRD IN A SERIES OF SOIRÉES HOSTED BY WASHINGTON COLUMNIST GEORGE WILL FOR HIS POLITICAL IDOL, RONALD REAGAN."

GEE, I HATE TO MISS THE FUN, BUT I'M PRETTY SURE I'M BUSY WHATEVER NIGHT HE'S HAVING IT.

"P.S.—ATTENDANCE AT THE SOIRÉE IS DE RIGUEUR."

DARN! WELL, C'EST LA VIE!

REDFERN! GOOD TO SEE YOU, BOY!

WELL, HELLO, SENATOR..

MEET THE GOVERNOR YET? GREAT GUY, JUST A REALLY GREAT GUY! ASKED ME ABOUT MY COMMITTEE, MY BILL, MY WIFE.. HELL, I GOT STROKED FROM HERE TO SUNDAY!

AFTER CARTER, YOU GOTTA LOVE IT, RIGHT? DAMN STRAIGHT! IF THERE'S ONE THING I LOVE MORE THAN GETTING BOMBED, IT'S GETTING STROKED!

STROKED AND BOMBED AND IT'S NOT EVEN 8:00! NOW THIS IS MY KINDA PARTY!

GLAD IT'S WORKING OUT SO WELL FOR YOU, SENATOR.

IT'S HARD TO BE-LIEVE— THE CREAM OF WASHINGTON SO-CIETY TOASTING A MAN WHO ONCE CO-STARRED WITH A CHIMPANZEE!

ISN'T SOCIAL MOBILITY WON-DERFUL? IT'S REALLY WHAT THIS COUNTRY IS ALL ABOUT.

WHAT A BREATH OF FRESH AIR THEY ARE! ELEGANCE, STYLE..

I KNOW. THESE PARTIES HAVE REALLY TURNED ME AROUND. I'M GOING TO WORK HARD FOR HIM IN CONGRESS!

BUT HARRY! YOU'RE A LIBERAL DEMOCRAT! WHAT HAPPENED TO YOUR PRINCI-PLES?

HE PUT THEM IN A BLIND TRUST RIGHT AFTER THE LAND-SLIDE.

MRS. REAGAN, I UNDERSTAND THE CARTERS WON'T GET OUT OF THE WHITE HOUSE EARLY SO YOU CAN REDEC-ORATE.

ISN'T THAT THE HEIGHT OF ARROGANCE? ESPECIALLY WITH SO MANY GOOD HOTELS NEARBY.

MRS. WILL AND I WOULD LIKE TO THANK YOU ALL FOR THE HONOR YOU DO US BY GRACING OUR SALON. AS A SIMPLE SUBUR-BAN SCRIBE, I MUST CON-FESS I'M SURPRISED BY MY NEW RESPECTABILITY.

PERHAPS I SHOULDN'T BE. AS HENRY DAVID THOREAU TOLD US, "IF ONE ADVANCES CONFIDENTLY IN THE DIRECTION OF HIS DREAMS, HE WILL MEET WITH A SUCCESS UNEXPECTED IN COMMON HOURS."

NOBODY EMBODIES THAT QUOTATION, AND SEVERAL OTHERS LIKE IT FROM MADISON, CHAUCER AND PLINY THE ELDER, MORE THAN RONALD REAGAN. PLEASE JOIN ME IN TOASTING OUR NEW.. OUR NEW.. RON? WHERE ARE YOU, RON?

ANYONE SEEN THE GOVERNOR?

HE'S UPSTAIRS TAKING A NAP, SIR. HE SAID HE'D BE DOWN FOR COFFEE.

I UNDERSTAND THAT WHILE I WAS UPSTAIRS NAPPING, GEORGE HERE OFFERED A DELIGHTFUL TOAST TO NANCY AND ME..

WELL, IF I MAY, I'D JUST LIKE TO RETURN THE COMPLIMENT. IT'S BEEN A LONG YEAR, BUT THROUGH IT ALL, GEORGE WILL HAS BEEN OF INVALUABLE SER-VICE — AS FRIEND, AS APOLO-GIST, AND NOW, AS HOST.

THERE ARE VERY FEW JOURNALISTS WHO WOULD FEEL IT WAS THEIR DUTY TO HELP US MEET THE PLAYERS IN THIS TOWN. BOTH NANCY AND I ARE MOST GRATE-FUL, AND WE HOPE, GEORGE, THAT YOU WILL HONOR US BY ACCEPTING THE POST OF TRANSITION TEAM SOCIAL DIRECTOR!

WHAT? OH, NO, GOVERNOR, I COULDN'T!

SURE, YOU COULD. YOU'VE COME THIS FAR.

GO FOR IT, GEORGE!

GENERAL HAIG, I'M SURE YOU'RE AS ANXIOUS AS WE ARE TO BRING THESE HEARINGS TO A CONCLUSION..

SPEAKING FOR THE DEMOCRATIC MINORITY OF THE COMMITTEE, I CAN ASSURE YOU THAT WE ARE NOT INTERESTED IN DWELLING ON YOUR ROLE IN WATERGATE ANY LONGER THAN NECESSARY.

WELL, THANKS, SENATOR, BUT FRANKLY, I CAN HACK IT WITHOUT ANYBODY PULLING PUNCHES. WE'RE HERE TO DETERMINE MY FITNESS, SO STOP WHIMPERING AND GIVE ME YOUR BEST SHOT!

OH..UM..OKAY, WHAT WAS YOUR ROLE?

NONE OF YOUR DAMN BUSINESS!

GENERAL, WHEN YOU BECAME NIXON'S CHIEF OF STAFF DURING THE WATERGATE CRISIS, WHAT DID YOU HOPE TO ACCOMPLISH?

AS I'VE ALREADY INDICATED, I SOUGHT TO PRESERVE THE CONSTITUTION.

ARE YOU SERIOUS? FIGHTING TO WITHHOLD EVIDENCE, ADVISING NIXON TO LIE, ORDERING THE SPECIAL PROSECUTOR FIRED—ALL THAT WAS TO PRESERVE THE CONSTITUTION?

AFFIRMATIVE.

=SIGH..=

GENERAL, IF YOU'RE CONFIRMED, DO YOU EXPECT TO BE DOING THE CONSTITUTION ANY FURTHER FAVORS?

NOT AT THIS POINT IN TIME.

GENERAL HAIG, I WONDER IF WE MIGHT TURN OUR ATTENTION NOW TO THE QUESTION OF THE NIXON PARDON.

ACCORDING TO PUBLISHED ACCOUNTS, YOU DISCUSSED THE PARDON WITH MR. FORD ON AUGUST 1, 1974, AGAIN LATER THAT NIGHT, AND ONCE MORE ON AUGUST 2. CORRECT?

YES, BUT THERE WAS NEVER ACTUALLY A QUID PRO QUO OFFER. I WAS SIMPLY DESCRIBING ONE POSSIBLE SCENARIO.

AND MR. FORD'S REACTION?

HE WAS APPALLED ALL THREE TIMES.

MOVING RIGHT ALONG, GENERAL, WE FIND THAT ANOTHER ONE OF YOUR CELEBRATED "MISSIONS" WAS DELIVERING TO THE FBI MR. KISSINGER'S REQUESTS FOR WIRETAPS ON HIS OWN STAFF..

MAY I ASSUME, GENERAL, THIS IS JUST ONE MORE STAIN OF WHICH YOU ARE ACTUALLY PROUD?

YOU MAY, SENATOR.

WE WERE FACED WITH A SECURITY CRISIS. OUR OPERATIONS WERE BEING COMPROMISED, SO ANYONE IN A POSITION TO KNOW ABOUT THE SECRET BOMBINGS IN CAMBODIA WAS SUSPECT. MY ONLY REGRET IS WE FAILED TO FIND ANY OF THE TRAITORS.

MAYBE IT WAS LEAKED BY THE VICTIMS.

WELL, WE THOUGHT OF THAT, BUT WE HAD NO LEGAL AUTHORITY TO PLACE TAPS IN CAMBODIA.

...AND WITH KEY SECOND-LEVEL POSTS STILL UNFILLED, THE TRANSITION PERIOD HAS BY NO MEANS ENDED WITH RONALD REAGAN'S SWEARING-IN CEREMONIES.

ON ANOTHER FRONT, HOWEVER, THE REAGANS SEEM TO HAVE GOTTEN OFF TO A ROARING START..

ONLY MINUTES AFTER THE INAUGURATION, MRS. REAGAN WAS WHISKED TO THE WHITE HOUSE WHERE SHE QUICKLY ASSUMED CONTROL OF THE HOUSEHOLD FROM THE FORMER FIRST LADY.

WHAT DO YOU WANT? GET OUT! IT'S MINE NOW!

UM.. SORRY, I JUST FORGOT MY PURSE.

MRS. REAGAN, WHEN DID YOU FIRST ACQUIRE YOUR HANDGUN?

IT WAS BACK WHEN RONNIE WAS TOURING THE COUNTRY FOR G.E.

HOLLYWOOD WAS JUST SWARMING WITH COMMUNISTS IN THOSE DAYS, AND RONNIE FELT I SHOULDN'T BE ALONE IN THE HOUSE WITHOUT PROTECTION.

BUT IT'S NO BIG DEAL. IT'S JUST THIS TINY LITTLE THING WITH VERY PRETTY MOTHER-OF-PEARL INLAY AND LITTLE DAISIES ETCHED ON THE BARREL.

AND WHAT DOES IT SHOOT?

TEENY-WEENY, LADYLIKE BULLETS.

GOOD EVENING. THERE WAS ANOTHER DRAMATIC BREAKTHROUGH TODAY IN THE CONTINUING SAGA OF THE AMERICAN HOSTAGES.

THE STATE DEPARTMENT HAS FORMALLY ANNOUNCED THAT NEGOTIATIONS HAVE JUST BEEN COMPLETED FOR THE RELEASE OF AN ADDITIONAL, 53RD HOSTAGE.

THE HOSTAGE'S IDENTITY IS STILL NOT KNOWN, BUT HE IS BEING REFERRED TO BY IRANIAN SOURCES AS "THE BALD SPY."

THE WHAT?

YOU KNOW A BALD SPY?

..AND SOURCES SAY THE 53RD HOSTAGE, KNOWN ONLY AS "THE BALD SPY," WILL BE FREE WITHIN HOURS.

NEGOTIATIONS FOR THE MYSTERY HOSTAGE'S RELEASE WERE SAID TO HAVE BEEN DIFFICULT, INVOLVING SEVERAL HOURS OF HAGGLING OVER EXACT TERMS.

A BREAKTHROUGH WAS FINALLY REACHED LATE LAST NIGHT WHEN U.S. OFFICIALS AGREED TO UNFREEZE ADDITIONAL IRANIAN ASSETS TOTALLING $300.

HOW MUCH?

IT WAS THE BEST WE COULD DO, BALD ONE.

GOOD EVENING. TODAY THE IDENTITY OF THE 53RD HOSTAGE WAS MADE KNOWN. HE IS FORMER U.S. AMBASSADOR DUKE..

I KNEW IT! I KNEW IT WAS UNCLE DUKE!

AT THE TEHRAN AIRPORT THIS MORNING, HE SPOKE WITH REPORTERS..

MR. DUKE, HOW DOES IT FEEL TO BE FREE?

GREAT. AND I WANT TO THANK THE THOUSANDS OF PEOPLE AROUND THE WORLD WHO PRESSURED IRAN FOR MY RELEASE. I'M CERTAIN THAT PUBLIC OUTRAGE WAS THE ONLY THING THAT STOOD BETWEEN ME AND A BRUTAL DEATH!

UH.. BUT NOBODY KNEW YOU WERE A HOSTAGE, SIR..

BALONEY. THERE WAS INTERNATIONAL PRESSURE. I COULD FEEL IT.

WHERE.. WHERE AM I?

DON'T BE ALARMED, MR. DUKE. YOU'RE IN A SPECIAL ARMY HOSPITAL. IN GERMANY. HOW DO YOU FEEL THIS MORNING?

ARE YOU FEELING ANXIOUS? A LITTLE DISORIENTED? THAT'S QUITE NORMAL. HOW ABOUT DEPRESSION? ANY DEPRESSION?

MR. DUKE, I CAN'T HELP YOU IF YOU WON'T LET ME. YOU'VE GOT TO OPEN UP, YOU'VE GOT TO TALK TO ME, DO YOU UNDERSTAND?

WHERE THE HELL IS MY WALLET?

GOOD. LET IT OUT. WHAT ELSE ARE YOU FEELING?

OKAY, DOC, WHEN DO I GET OUT OF THIS DUMP?

IN TIME, MR. DUKE, ALL IN TIME. YOU'VE BEEN THROUGH QUITE AN ORDEAL..

LOOK, I'M FINE, DOC. JUST GIVE ME MY PANTS BACK AND I'LL BE ON MY WAY!

LET'S TALK FOR A WHILE FIRST, OKAY? TELL ME A LITTLE ABOUT YOUR CAPTORS.

AHMAD AND ASIF? GOOD MEN, BOTH OF THEM. IF THEY HADN'T BEEN KEEPING AN EYE ON ME, THE CIA WOULD HAVE WASTED ME MONTHS AGO!

THAT REMINDS ME, I PROMISED I'D CALL THE GUYS AND LET THEM KNOW I'M OKAY..

TEXTBOOK CASE.

I CONCUR.

MR. DUKE, I'M AFRAID WE'RE GOING TO HAVE TO KEEP YOU WITH US FOR A FEW DAYS FOR OBSERVATION.

WHAT THE HELL FOR? I'M FINE, DOC!

YOU'RE SUFFERING FROM WHAT WE CALL THE "STOCKHOLM SYNDROME," WHICH IS THE TENDENCY OF A HOSTAGE TO SYMPATHIZE WITH HIS TORMENTORS.

TORMENTORS? ARE YOU CRAZY? HOW DO YOU EXPLAIN ALL THE GOOD TIMES? THE SOCCER GAMES BEHIND THE COMPOUND? THE LATE NIGHTS OF DRINKING?

ALL TYPICAL ELEMENTS OF THE CAPTOR-HOSTAGE RELATIONSHIP.

THE SAILING VACATION IN GREECE?

LESS TYPICAL, BUT NOT UNHEARD OF.

LET'S GO BACK TO THE BEGINNING OF YOUR CAPTIVITY, SHALL WE, MR. DUKE? AT LAST REPORT YOU WERE FACING A PREDAWN FIRING SQUAD.

RIGHT. AT THAT POINT, NEGOTIATIONS HAD KIND OF BOGGED DOWN. I WAS FORCED TO MAKE A LAST-DITCH OFFER OF $250,000, WHICH IT TURNED OUT WAS THE GOING RATE FOR A STAY OF EXECUTION.

IT WAS AN INCREDIBLE RIP-OFF, BUT I FIGURED, WHAT THE HELL, I'D BE LONG GONE BY THE TIME MY CHECK BOUNCED. UNFORTUNATELY, THEY LOCKED ME UP IN A HOTEL AS INSURANCE.

OKAY, BALD ONE, BACK TO THE ROOF.

I CAN'T UNDERSTAND IT. THEY MUST HAVE FROZEN MY ASSETS.

OKAY, BALD ONE, BACK TO THE ROOF.

LOOK, FELLAHS, I REALLY THINK YOU'RE OVERREACTING. WHY RISK WAR WITH THE U.S. OVER ONE LOUSY BAD CHECK?

I MEAN, IF YOU'RE SO BENT ON CREATING AN INTERNATIONAL INCIDENT, WHY DON'T YOU JUST SEIZE THE WHOLE UNITED STATES EMBASSY?

YOU SAID WHAT?

I WAS JUST KIDDING, FOR GOD'S SAKE..

THE NEXT DAY ALL HELL BROKE LOOSE..

THE EMBASSY'S BEEN SEIZED!

HUH?

IT'S YOUR LUCKY DAY, BALD ONE. WE'VE BEEN TOLD TO KEEP YOU ALIVE AS A BARGAINING CHIP!

GOOD PLAN. YOU WON'T REGRET IT.

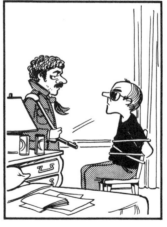

SO WHAT DO YOU WANT TO DO WHILE THEY NEGOTIATE?

I DUNNO. WHY DON'T WE GO GRAB A BEER?

THE MONTHS DRAGGED BY..

GUARD!

KEEP IT DOWN, BALD ONE! I'M BUSY!

I THOUGHT YOU WERE GOING TO GET ME SOME CIGARETTES!

I SAID, QUIET! I'M TRYING TO STUDY!

WHAT DO YOU MEAN QUIET? I NEED THOSE CIGARETTES NOW! AND WHERE'S THAT NEW PICTURE? I'M SICK OF THIS DAMN ICON! DO YOU HEAR ME, GUARD?

FOR CRYING OUT LOUD, BALD ONE! I'VE GOT FINALS TOMORROW!

GET ME SOMETHING CLASSY, OKAY? YOU KNOW, LIKE A LEROY NEIMAN SPORTING PRINT!

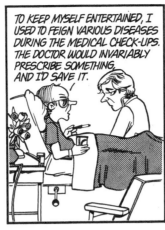

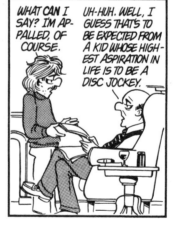

LOOK, DAD, IF YOU ASKED ME TO COME HOME JUST SO YOU COULD GLOAT, I THINK I'LL BE ON MY..

CAN'T TAKE IT, HUH? THE KID WHO GLOATED OVER WATERGATE FOR FIVE YEARS?

YEAH, WELL, WHO CACKLED WITH GLEE WHEN NIXON BEAT McGOVERN?

WHO BECAME INSUFFERABLE OVER VIETNAMI-ZATION?

THAT WASN'T AS BAD AS YOUR GLOATING OVER THE CAMBODIAN BLOODBATH!

ME? THAT WAS YOU!

IT WAS? ..YOU SURE?

UM.. I THINK SO. WHOSE FAULT DID THAT TURN OUT TO BE?

OFF TO WORK ALREADY, SWEETEST?

I'M AFRAID SO, DEAR. I HAVE TO GET READY FOR THE COMMITTEE'S HEARINGS ON THE NEW TAX CUTS TODAY.

WHAT A DREARY MESS THE WHITE HOUSE HAS HANDED US. IT'S NOTHING BUT AN-OTHER WINDFALL FOR THE WEALTHY. AS IF THE RICH DIDN'T ALREADY HAVE ENOUGH WAYS TO AVOID PAYING TAXES!

WELL, GIVE THEM HECK, DEAR. BUT DO TRY TO KEEP IT IN PERSPECTIVE.

WHAT DO YOU MEAN, DICK?

DON'T FORGET WE'RE RICH.

DON'T WORRY, DEAR. I'LL TRY TO LEAVE IN A SAFETY NET.

WELL, I GUESS EVERYONE'S HERE. WHO'S OUR FIRST WITNESS TODAY, DEAR?

A MR. SLACK-MEYER. HE JUST JOINED THE COUN-CIL OF ECONOMIC ADVISERS.

REP. DAVENPORT   REP. GE

SLACKMEYER? HMM.. DON'T THINK I KNOW THAT NAME.

HE'S AN EXPERT IN TAX SHELTERS AND MONEY FUNDS.

REP. DAVENPORT   REP. G

HE LOOKS A LITTLE NERVOUS. HAS HE EVER TESTIFIED BEFORE?

YES. ONCE DURING THE TRUMAN AD-MINISTRATION.

REP. DAVENPORT

POOR DEAR. I BETTER GO WARM HIM UP.

UM.. LACEY, TRY NOT TO GIVE AWAY THE QUES-TIONS THIS TIME, OKAY?

REP. DAVENPORT   REP. G

MR. SLACKMEYER? I'M MRS. DAVENPORT, AND I'D LIKE TO WELCOME YOU TO OUR LITTLE COMMITTEE HEARING..

OH.. WELL, THANK YOU, CONGRESS-WOMAN.

WE'RE ALL LOOKING FORWARD TO YOUR TESTIMONY WITH SUCH INTEREST!

A FRIENDLY WORD OF WARNING, THOUGH. IF YOU INDULGE IN THE KIND OF META-PHYSICAL MUSH WE'VE BEEN HEARING FROM SO MANY OF YOUR COLLEAGUES LATELY, I CAN PROMISE YOU A VERY, VERY LONG AFTERNOON.

YOU CAN?

AFTERWARDS, OF COURSE, WE HOPE YOU'LL JOIN US FOR TEA AT MY OFFICE.

MADAM CHAIRWOMAN, IT IS WITH GREAT CONFIDENCE THAT I RECOMMEND TO THIS COMMITTEE THE ADMINISTRATION'S ECONOMIC RECOVERY PROGRAM.

I BELIEVE THAT IN THE VERY NEAR FUTURE, AMERICANS CAN EXPECT TO SEE AN ECONOMY IN WHICH INFLATION IS LOW, PRODUCTIVITY HIGH, THE FEDERAL BUDGET BALANCED, AND THE DOLLAR MIGHTY ONCE AGAIN!

HOW DO WE PROPOSE TO DO THIS? WELL, SIMPLY BY ADDING THREE ANNUAL TAX CUTS TO A TIGHT MONEY POLICY, A BURST OF DEREGULATION, A MASSIVE MILITARY BUILDUP, AND A SET OF CHANGING EXPECTATIONS.

TAKEN TOGETHER..

DON'T FORGET THE EYE OF A NEWT.

MR. SLACKMEYER, WOULDN'T YOU AGREE THAT THE MOST INDEFENSIBLE ASPECT OF YOUR TAX CUT PROPOSALS IS THE UNCONSCIONABLE WAY IN WHICH THEY FAVOR THE RICH?

NO, SIR, I CERTAINLY WOULD NOT. IF WE'RE GOING TO AVOID AN ECONOMIC ANZIO, THEN WE HAVE TO MOVE BOLDLY. WE CAN'T AFFORD TO ENGAGE IN A FISCAL BATTLE OF MIDWAY WITHOUT OUR CAPTAINS OF INDUSTRY!

FROM PAST EXPERIENCE, WE KNOW THAT THE WELL-HEELED ARE THE ONLY CLASS THAT CAN BE DEPENDED ON TO PUT THEIR TAX CUTS INTO SAVINGS AND INVESTMENTS!

AND THE POOR?

STUDIES SHOW THEY TEND TO BLOW IT ALL AT THE TRACK.

GOOD EVENING. TODAY THE FUROR CONTINUED OVER PRESIDENT REAGAN'S RECENT STATEMENT THAT THE ONLY LESSON OF VIETNAM WAS TO "NEVER ENTER INTO A WAR YOU DON'T INTEND TO WIN."

WITH THE MEMORY OF 210,000 U.S. CASUALTIES STILL VIVID, MILLIONS OF SHOCKED AMERICANS EXPRESSED OUTRAGE OVER THE DISCLOSURE THAT THEIR GOVERNMENT NEVER HAD ANY INTENTION OF WINNING THE VIETNAM WAR.

Vietnam 1959-1973

I'M ROLAND HEDLEY. AS CRIES OF "NEVER AGAIN" RING OUT ACROSS THE COUNTRY TONIGHT, JOIN ME AS WE TAKE A LOOK INTO OUR OWN FRONT YARD.. FOR A WAR WE CAN WIN!

BROUGHT TO YOU BY HERTZ, WHERE THE WINNERS RENT..

EL SALVADOR

ONE FOR THE GIPPER 1981-?

IN THE WAKE OF MR. REAGAN'S STARTLING DISCLOSURE THAT THE U.S. NEVER INTENDED TO WIN THE VIETNAM WAR, SCORES OF VETERANS HAVE COME FORWARD TO CONFIRM HIS CLAIM. SGT. LENNY McCOVEY RECALLS.

VIETNAM

I REMEMBER ONCE NEAR DA NANG, WE HAD THIS GOOK UNIT PINNED DOWN IN THE OPEN. WE WERE ABOUT TO CALL IN SOME SKYRAIDERS FOR A NAPALM DROP WHEN THE C.O. JUST CALLED OFF THE OPERATION.

DID THAT HAPPEN OFTEN?

HELL, YES. EVERY TIME WE HAD A REAL CHANCE OF STICKING IT TO CHARLIE, WORD WOULD COME DOWN THE U.S. WASN'T SERIOUS ABOUT WINNING IN VIETNAM.

INCREDIBLE. HOW MANY OTHER G.I.'S KNEW ABOUT THIS?

PRETTY MUCH ALL 500,000 OF US.

WHETHER THE U.S. MEANT TO WIN THE VIETNAM WAR OR NOT, TODAY THERE IS GROWING PRESSURE TO FIND A WAR WE CAN WIN. U.S. STRATEGIST ABE LEVIN EXPLAINS HOW EL SALVADOR WAS SELECTED!

IT WASN'T EASY. WE'D BEEN LOOKING FOR A PLACE TO DRAW THE LINE FOR WEEKS, BUT THERE JUST WEREN'T ANY CIVIL WARS ON THE FRONT PAGE. FINALLY, SOME GUY IN RESEARCH HIT ON EL SALVADOR.

IT WAS PERFECT. SMALL, CLOSE TO HOME, AND THE RIGHT SIDE WAS ALREADY WINNING. WE HIT IT HARD. WITHIN DAYS, WE'D TURNED EL SALVADOR INTO A METAPHOR FOR THE GEOPOLITICAL STRUGGLE BETWEEN THE SUPERPOWERS!

AND THE RUSSIANS AGREED WITH YOUR CHOICE?

WELL, NO, THEY WANTED SOME PERSIAN GULF STATE, BUT WE PUT OUR FOOT DOWN.

THE JUNTA. AN UNEASY COALITION OF CIVILIANS AND COMIC-OPERA COLONELS, HEADED, CURIOUSLY, BY A FORMER TORTURE VICTIM, JOSÉ DUARTE. RECENTLY I CHATTED WITH DUARTE ABOUT HIS TWO MISSING FINGERS.

MR. PRESIDENT, GIVEN THAT YOU YOURSELF WERE ONCE MUTILATED BY THE MILITARY, WHY ARE YOU WILLING TO DO BUSINESS WITH THEM?

WELL, IT TURNED OUT IT WAS ALL JUST A MISUNDERSTANDING.

BESIDES, MY PEOPLE LOVE ME FOR MY PAST SUFFERING. I AM ONE OF THEM. HAVING BEEN TO THE TORTURE CHAMBERS, I KNOW WHAT IT'S LIKE TO LIVE IN THE SHADOW OF FEAR AND PAIN.

BUT ISN'T THAT REALLY JUST A POLITICAL GIMMICK, MR. PRESIDENT?

YOU'RE TOUGH, MY FRIEND.

EL SALVADOR. IS IT REALLY "ONE WE CAN WIN"? FURTHERMORE, WHAT CONSTITUTES WINNING? WITH HELP FROM AN INTERPRETER, WE TALKED TO SECRETARY OF STATE ALEXANDER HAIG..

SECRETARY HAIG, WHAT IS THE CHIEF U.S. OBJECTIVE IN EL SALVADOR TODAY?

TO IMPACT THE JUNTA MILITARILY, SO AS TO HEARTS-AND-MINDS THE INDIGENOUS ELEMENTS.

SECRETARY HAIG SAYS THE GOAL IS TO WIN LOCAL SUPPORT FOR THE JUNTA BY GIVING THEM MORE ARMS.

I SEE. AND HOW DO YOU PROPOSE TO GET CONGRESSIONAL LEADERS TO GO ALONG WITH THIS?

WE PLAN TO SCENARIO THEM ROSILY.

SECRETARY HAIG SAYS..

I THINK I GOT IT.

HEY..

WHAT?

I THINK I JUST MADE A DECISION.

WHAT SORT OF DECISION?

I.. I THINK I WANT TO GET MARRIED.

THAT'S GREAT. TO WHOM?

NO, I'M SERIOUS. SOMETHING JUST CLICKED. GET YOUR COAT.

COMING UP: THE EVENING NEWS..

BUT FIRST, TELETYPE MACHINE SOUND EFFECTS!

CLACKITY CLACK! CLACKITY..

GOOD EVENING. TODAY THE SENATE FINALLY COMPLETED THE CONFIRMATION HEARINGS OF CHESTER P. BIFFLE, NOMINEE FOR THE POST OF DEPUTY SECRETARY OF STATE FOR COLD WAR AFFAIRS.

THE HEARINGS HAD BEEN DELAYED WHILE A FEDERAL GRAND JURY DELIBERATED EXTORTION CHARGES AGAINST BIFFLE. ALTHOUGH HE WAS FINALLY EXONERATED, THOSE CHARGES WERE REPEATED TODAY BY SIX DIFFERENT WITNESSES.

OTHER WITNESSES ACCUSED BIFFLE OF CONFLICT OF INTEREST, MOB CONNECTIONS, WAR CRIMES, OBSTRUCTION OF JUSTICE AND SODOMY, BUT IN SWORN TESTIMONY, FBI OFFICIALS CONFIRMED THAT BIFFLE WAS INNOCENT UNTIL PROVEN GUILTY.

TURNING TO HIS QUALIFICATIONS, THE COMMITTEE DETERMINED THAT BIFFLE'S FAMILIARITY WITH FOREIGN AFFAIRS DID NOT EXTEND BEYOND HIS SUBSCRIPTION TO "NATIONAL GEOGRAPHIC." HE WAS UNABLE TO NAME THE LEADERS OF JAPAN, FRANCE, GERMANY OR THE U.S.S.R.

HOWEVER, FOLLOWING BIFFLE'S TESTIMONY, SENATOR JESSE HELMS PRAISED THE FORMER REAGAN FUNDRAISER, SAYING, "NOBODY'S GOT A MONOPOLY ON INTELLIGENCE OR VIRTUE." ADDED SENATOR CHARLES PERCY, "HE SEEMS NICE ENOUGH."

BIFFLE'S CONFIRMATION BY THE FULL SENATE IS EXPECTED TOMORROW.

WHEW!

THAT'S JUST PERFECT! HOW MUCH WOULD IT COST?

WELL, THE IRIS IS FLOWN IN FROM HOLLAND, SO IT WOULD BE CLOSE TO $65 AN ARRANGEMENT.

OH, DEAR.. I'M AFRAID THAT'S MUCH TOO EXPENSIVE..

OH? HOW MUCH WAS MADAM PREPARED TO SPEND?

ABOUT EIGHT DOLLARS A TABLE?

EIGHT DOLLARS?

I'M DREAMING, AREN'T I?

PERHAPS MADAM WOULD LIKE US TO ARRANGE SOME DANDELIONS FOR HER.

G.B. Trudeau

HI, BABE. HOW'D THE INVITATIONS TURN OUT?

RICK, THEY'RE ABSOLUTELY BEAUTIFUL.

ENGRAVED TYPE, LINEN PAPER, RETURN CARDS— PRETTY CLASSY FOR A LAST-MINUTE JOB, WOULDN'T YOU SAY?

HMM.. NOT BAD, BUT WHO'S THIS "BICK REDFERN" YOU'RE MARRYING?

BICK?

GOOD OL' BICK. I THOUGHT HE'D NEVER GET MARRIED.

AARGH!

— G.B. Trudeau

"BICK"! HOW COULD THEY SPELL YOUR NAME "BICK"?

OH, DON'T WORRY ABOUT IT, JOANIE..

DON'T WORRY ABOUT IT? YOU DON'T CARE THAT YOUR NAME'S MISSPELLED ON YOUR OWN WEDDING INVITATION?!

I'M IN THE NEWSPAPER BUSINESS. I'M USED TO TYPOS.

WELL, I'M NOT! AND I DON'T WANT ALL MY FRIENDS CALLING YOU "BICK" AT THE WEDDING.

IF THERE IS A WEDDING. LOOKS LIKE THEY ALSO LEFT OFF THE DATE.

I CAN'T STAND IT..

NOW, THAT'S A PROBLEM. WE COULD HAVE RELATIVES DROPPING IN ON US ALL SUMMER.

G.B. Trudeau

I CAN'T BELIEVE IT. HOW COULD THEY LEAVE THE DATE OFF, TOO?

LOOK, IT'S NO BIG DEAL. WE'LL JUST INCLUDE ERRATUM SLIPS. IT'S DONE ALL THE TIME.

NOT WITH A WEDDING INVITATION, IT ISN'T!

OKAY, THEN, WE'LL JUST CALL EVERYONE WITH THE CORRECTIONS AFTER THEY GET THE INVITATIONS.

PHONE IN THE CORRECTIONS? ARE YOU SERIOUS, RICK?

SURE, WHY NOT?

"HI. THERE'S BEEN A CHANGE. THE GROOM'S NAME IS NOW RICK."

BEATS HAVING TO RETURN MONOGRAMMED STUFF LATER.

G.B. Trudeau

WHO COULD BE CALLING AT SUCH A DREADFUL HOUR?

I'LL TAKE CARE OF IT, DEAREST. GO BACK TO SLEEP.. *RING!*

HELLO?

DICK? THAD! HOLD ON TO YOUR HAT, OLD BOY! A BACHMAN'S WARBLER WAS SIGHTED TODAY OUT AT LOVE POINT!

LACEY! SWEETEST! A *BACHMAN'S WAR-BLER* WAS SPOTTED NEAR THE CHESAPEAKE!

THAT'S VERY EXCITING, DEAR. I CAN'T WAIT TO DISCUSS IT IN THE MORNING.

WE'LL BE THERE IN TEN MINUTES!

A BACHMAN'S WARBLER! I CAN'T BELIEVE IT! WHAT A WAY TO MAKE IT INTO THE 700 CLUB!

THE *WHAT*, DEAR?

IT'S AN ELITE GROUP OF BIRD-ERS WHO HAVE SEEN 700 NORTH AMERICAN BIRDS! IF I SEE THE WARBLER, MY LIFE LIST WILL GO OVER THE TOP! YOU *HAVE* TO BE THERE!

DICK, IT'S 3:00 A.M. CAN'T IT WAIT?

WAIT? LACEY, I'VE BEEN WAITING TO SEE A BACH-MAN MY WHOLE CAREER! I'M 70 YEARS OLD! THE BACH-MAN WARBLER IS NEARLY EXTINCT!

LET'S NOT BE MELODRAMATIC, DEAR.

BUT DON'T YOU SEE? IT'S ONLY A MATTER OF TIME BEFORE ONE OF US GOES!

WILL YOU *LOOK* AT THAT SUNRISE! WHAT A DAY FOR BIRDING! I'M SO GLAD YOU CAME, SWEETEST!

WELL, NOW THAT I'M UP, I MUST SAY I'M LOOK-ING FORWARD TO OUR LITTLE EXCURSION.

WELL, I DON'T THINK YOU'LL REGRET IT, LOVED ONE. THE REWARDS OF BIRDING ARE CONSIDER-ABLE INDEED!

WITH A LITTLE PATIENCE AND A GOOD PAIR OF EYES, *ANY-BODY* CAN FIND DELIGHTS IN THE NATURAL WORLD WHICH BOTH THRILL AND ASTOUND!

OF COURSE, PART OF IT'S KNOWING WHERE TO SET UP.

I WAS ABOUT TO SAY.

HMM.. NO SIGN OF THE WARBLER. I HOPE IT WASN'T A FALSE IDENTI-FICATION.

IT'S BEEN FIVE HOURS, DICK. MAYBE HE'S GONE.

MAYBE, DEAR HEART, BUT I'D PREFER TO ERR ON THE SIDE OF CAUTION. A TRUE BIRDER KNOWS THE VALUE OF PATIENCE.

I GUESS IT'S ALWAYS BEEN THAT WAY WITH ME. EVEN IN GRAMMAR SCHOOL, MY PEERS SEEMED TO SENSE I WAS DESTINED FOR A LIFE OF BIRDING.

HOW'S THAT, DEAR?

THEY USED TO CALL ME "THE BEAK."

KIDS ARE SO PERCEPTIVE THAT WAY.

AHA! I GOT THE LITTLE RASCAL!

HOW EXCITING, DEAR! ARE YOU SURE IT'S A BACHMAN'S WARBLER?

ONLY ONE WAY TO TELL FOR SURE, MY SWEET! I'LL HAVE TO CONFIRM WITH A BIRD CALL!

TWEE! TWEE CURRY! SHE-WACKA-TOO! TWEE! TWEE CURRY! SHE-WACKA-TOO! SHE-WACKA-TOO!

CHIRP!

>SIGH<..

WHAT'D HE SAY, DEAR? IS IT HIM?

I'M SORRY YOU DIDN'T SEE YOUR WARBLER, DICK.

IT DOESN'T MATTER, DEAR. THE TRUE BIRDER CARES MORE ABOUT BEING OUT IN THE SWEET, SPRING AIR THAN ADDING TO HIS LIST!

BESIDES, HE'S ALMOST ALWAYS REWARDED BY SOME SPECIAL MOMENT! HARDLY A DAY GOES BY WHEN I DON'T COME UPON A SONGBIRD POURING FORTH, IN SHELLEY'S WORDS, HIS "FULL HEART IN PROFUSE STRAINS OF UNPRE-MEDITATED ART."

DO ALL BIRDERS HAVE BEDROOM EYES, DEAR HEART?

HEE, HEE! WHO SAYS THIS DAY WAS A LOSS?

I CAN'T BELIEVE THIS HOUSE, MOM..!

WELL, IT'S THE DREAM HOME WE'VE ALWAYS WANTED, MARK.

BUT WHY DO YOU NEED SUCH A BIG PLACE?

WELL, NOW THAT YOUR FATHER'S WITH THE AD-MINISTRATION, WE DO A LOT OF ENTERTAINING, DEAR.

NATURALLY, WE'VE HAD TO TAKE ON A FEW DOMESTICS, BUT YOU KNOW HOW MUCH YOUR FATHER LIKES CREATING JOBS.

ILLEGAL ALIENS, I ASSUME,

JUST THE KITCHEN HELP. THEY DO SUCH MARVELOUS THINGS WITH CHICKEN.

SO AREN'T YOU GOING TO ASK HOW THINGS HAVE BEEN GOING?

I THINK I KNOW, DAD..

MOM SAYS THAT SINCE REAGAN'S BUDGET PASSED, YOU'VE BEEN INSUF-FERABLE.

NOW, DEAR, I DIDN'T PUT IT QUITE LIKE THAT.

HEE, HEE!

I HOPE YOU'RE HAPPY, DAD. I HOPE YOU'RE HAPPY KNOWING YOU PLAYED A KEY ROLE IN ROLLING BACK 50 YEARS OF SOCIAL PROGRESS!

CACKLE!

HE'S HAPPY.

NOW, DEAR, YOU PROMISED NOT TO GLOAT MARK'S FIRST DAY HOME.

HI, JIM, WHAT BRINGS YOU OVER HERE?

I NEED TO SEE THE PRESIDENT. MY INITIATIVES TO USE FEDERAL LANDS KEEP GETTING BLOCKED BY THE COURTS!

"ONLY YOU CAN PREVENT FORESTS"

SCENE 8 TAKE 2

I CAN'T UNDERSTAND THOSE PEOPLE! WHEN THE LORD RETURNS, HE'S NOT GOING TO BE INTERESTED IN TREES! HE'LL WANT TO KNOW WHY WE HAVEN'T MORE FULLY EXPLOITED THE NATURAL RESOURCES HE GAVE US!

INTERESTING THEOLOGICAL THEORY, JIM. YOU CAN TAKE IT UP WITH R.R. AS SOON AS HE GETS BACK FROM RIDING IN THE PARK.

RIDING IN THE PARK? WHY ON EARTH IS HE DOING THAT?

WELL, IT'S SUCH A NICE DAY OUT..

MAYBE TO AN ENVIRONMENTAL EXTREMIST.

BOY, DOESN'T THIS PLACE LOOK SPIFFY, ED? IT JUST SHOWS WHAT CAN BE DONE WITH A FEW PRIVATE CONTRIBUTIONS!

ACTUALLY, SIR, IT DIDN'T QUITE WORK OUT THAT WAY..

"HOME SWEET HOME"

SCENE 3 TAKE 18

WHAT DO YOU MEAN? WE TURNED DOWN THE $50,000 FOR DECORATING AUTHORIZED BY CONGRESS.

YES, SIR, BUT THE $825,000 DONATED BY YOUR FRIENDS, MOST OF WHOM ARE IN THE 50% TAX BRACKET, WAS TAX-DEDUCTIBLE..

SO INSTEAD OF SAVING THE GOVERNMENT $50,000, YOUR REDECORATING IS ACTUALLY COSTING THE TREASURY MORE THAN $300,000 IN LOST REVENUES.

PWAT!

GOSH.. HOW IRONIC!

WELL, THE IMPORTANT THING IS AMERICA CAN BE PROUD OF YOUR LIVING QUARTERS AGAIN, SIR.

..SO HARPO TURNED TO CAGNEY, WHO WAS STILL IN TAILS, AND JUST LET HIM HAVE IT WITH THE SELTZER BOTTLE!

"BEDTIME FOR CONGRESS"

SCENE 1 TAKE 1

HA, HA! HA, HA! THAT'S GREAT!

HA, HA! VERY GOOD, SIR!

UH..MR. PRESIDENT, I WONDER IF WE COULD GET BACK TO OUR TAX CUT PROPOSALS..

GEE, TIP, I THINK ED CAN HANDLE THAT FOR YOU, CAN'T YOU, ED?

YES, SIR. DON'T GIVE IT ANOTHER THOUGHT.

SO ANYWAY, JIMMY JUST ABOUT HIT THE ROOF!

HA, HA, HA!

SIR, TELL THEM THE ONE ABOUT ERROL FLYNN AND THE WAITRESS!

ISN'T ZONKER COMING DOWN FOR BREAKFAST?

HE'LL BE DOWN. HIS TRAINER JUST WENT UP TO GET HIM.

HIS TRAINER?

BERNIE. EVER SINCE HE HELPED ZONK WIN THE JACK FORD TANNING AWARD, HE'S BEEN FANATICAL ABOUT KEEPING HIM ON HIS SCHEDULE!

BUT IT'S RAINING TODAY.

THAT WON'T STOP BERNIE!

OKAY, CHAMP, GET THE LEAD OUT!

HUH?

YES, THIS IS ZONKER HARRIS.

MR. HARRIS, THIS IS NELSON COHN. I'M AN INVESTIGATIVE REPORTER FOR "TANNER'S WORLD."

"TANNER'S WORLD"? NO KIDDING?

YES, SIR. I'M CALLING ABOUT YOUR PRESS RELEASE, IN WHICH YOU CLAIM TO BE RETIRING BECAUSE OF YOUR "STUDIES"..

WELL, I'VE BEEN CHECKING AROUND, AND YOU HAVEN'T GONE TO CLASS IN MONTHS! YET YOU'RE RETIRING AT FAME'S DOORSTEP TO DEVOTE YOUR LIFE TO SCHOOL! IT DOESN'T ADD UP, MR. HARRIS. SOMETHING SMELLS, AND I'M GOING TO GET TO THE BOTTOM OF IT!

FANTASTIC! WHAT ISSUE WILL THIS BE IN?

IS IT THE MOB? IF YOU CAN'T TALK, JUST CLEAR YOUR THROAT.

GBTrudeau

IT JUST DOESN'T WASH, HARRIS. A WORLD-CLASS TANNIST DOESN'T RETIRE TO STUDY DENTISTRY!

OKAY, LOOK, I'LL LEVEL WITH YOU. IT WASN'T REALLY MY STUDIES..

THEN WHAT WAS IT? YOU HAD EVERYTHING GOING FOR YOU! YOU COULD HAVE HAD THE TITLE, YOU COULD HAVE BEATEN HAMILTON, YOU..

WHAT?

EXCUSE ME, MR. COHN, BUT ONE DOES NOT "BEAT" GEORGE HAMILTON! TAN-MASTER HAMILTON IS THE STANDARD AGAINST WHICH ALL OTHER TANS ARE MEASURED!

OH..SORRY.. I FORGOT YOU STUDIED UNDER HIM..

I THINK THIS CONVERSATION IS OVER, DON'T YOU?

GBTrudeau

YOU REALLY THINK ZONKER'S MAKING A BIG MISTAKE BY RETIRING, DON'T YOU, BERNIE?

DARN RIGHT I DO. IT'S JUST UNCONSCIONABLE. HE'S LETTING A LOT OF PEOPLE DOWN.

WELL, I WOULDN'T BE SO QUICK TO JUDGE, BERNIE. ZONKER'S PAID HIS DUES. HE SWEATED AND BAKED FOR FOUR YEARS OUT ON THAT CIRCUIT, AND HE WON A LOT OF NEW FANS FOR THE SEDENTARY ARTS.

I THINK HE'S ENTITLED TO A CHANGE NOW, BERNIE, AND HE'S ALSO ENTITLED TO OUR SUPPORT. HE'S GOT A BRAND-NEW LIFE AHEAD OF HIM, AND I ADMIRE HIS COURAGE FOR FACING IT SQUARELY!

..AND IT LOOKS LIKE ANOTHER CLEAR, SUNNY WEEKEND, JACK!

MY GOD.. WHAT HAVE I DONE?..

ZONKER, I KNOW HOW YOU MUST FEEL, I REALLY DO. IT CAN'T BE EASY GIVING UP YOUR LIFE'S WORK..

BUT YOU CAN'T SPEND THE REST OF YOUR LIFE IN A STATE OF PRE-CANCEROUS REPOSE. YOU HAVE TO MOVE ON, DEVELOP SOME NEW INTERESTS!

THERE'S NO SHAME IN IT, ZONKER! YOU HAVE TO STOP FEELING GUILTY! YOU HAVE TO STOP TEARING YOURSELF APART OVER THIS THING!

ZZZZ..

THAT'S IT. TRY TO GET SOME SLEEP.

GBTrudeau

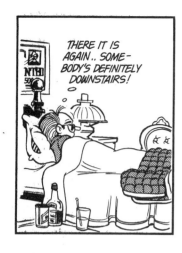

THERE IT IS AGAIN.. SOMEBODY'S DEFINITELY DOWNSTAIRS!

HMM.. I COULD BE WALKING INTO A TRAP.. I BETTER SHOOT FIRST, ASK QUESTIONS LATER..

BLAM! BLAM! BLAM! BLAM!

HELLO? ANYONE THERE?

>GURGLE..<

ONE MOVE AND YOU'RE A DEAD MAN!

DUKE..DON'T SHOOT..IT'S ME..>COUGH< BRENNER..

BRENNER! WHAT THE HELL ARE YOU DOING HERE?

YOU.. >GASP< YOU..

WHOA..I REALLY WINGED YOU GOOD, DIDN'T I? SORRY ABOUT THAT, KID., ACCIDENTS HAPPEN..

YOU..YOU TRIED TO KILL ME!

DON'T BE SILLY. I THOUGHT YOU WERE A RACCOON. WANT A BEER?

HERE..USE THIS TOWEL AS A TOURNIQUET.. YOU'RE BLEEDING LIKE A STUCK PIG..

YOU.. >COUGH< YOU.. TRIED TO KILL ME, MAN..

WILL YOU GET OFF THAT, BRENNER? I TOLD YOU, I THOUGHT YOU WERE A RACCOON!

YOU TRIED TO MURDER ME, MAN..

WHY YOU PATHETIC LITTLE PUP! DO YOU REALLY THINK I WOULD JEOPARDIZE MY CAREER BY WASTING A PUNK LIKE YOU? DON'T FLATTER YOURSELF, JACK!

MURDERER.

LOOK, I GOTTA GET SOME SHUT-EYE. YOU WANT AN AMBULANCE OR WHAT?

PLEASE.

MURDERER!

HEY, HOLD IT DOWN, WILLYA KID? I'M ON THE PHONE!

GOOD EVENING, ASPEN AMBULANCE.

HELLO, LES? DUKE HERE. LOOK, WE'VE HAD A LITTLE ACCIDENT OUT AT THE HOUSE. BRENNER'S TAKEN A SLUG. HE'S BLEEDING ALL OVER THE PLACE.

OKAY, HOLD ON, DUKE. I'LL SEND A WAGON OUT RIGHT AWAY.

GOOD. LISTEN, LES, THIS IS KIND OF A SENSITIVE MATTER. I'M THINKING ABOUT GETTING BACK INTO POLITICS, SO I'D APPRECIATE YOUR DISCRETION.

I HEAR YOU, OL' BUDDY. I'LL HAVE THE GUYS USE THE BACK ROAD.

GREAT. SAY, COULD YOU HAVE THEM SWING BY AND PICK ME UP A PIZZA?

NO PROBLEM. YOU WANT IT WITH EVERYTHING?

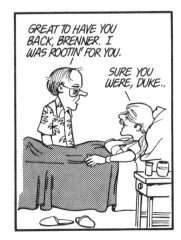

TRY TO KEEP THE QUESTIONS BRIEF, LIEUTENANT. THE BOY'S BEEN THROUGH A TERRIBLE ORDEAL.

MR. BRENNER, WHAT HAPPENED AT MR. DUKE'S HOUSE TONIGHT?

I JUST DROPPED BY TO PICK UP MY STEREO. I WAS WALKING THROUGH THE DEN WHEN SUDDENLY, WITHOUT WARNING, DUKE OPENS FIRE!

I SEE. THEN WHAT?

THEN HE STUMBLES DOWNSTAIRS, TURNS ON THE LIGHT, AND SEES IT'S ME!

I WAS SHOCKED, OF COURSE.

WHAT'D HE SAY?

"GIVE ME ONE GOOD REASON WHY I SHOULDN'T FINISH YOU OFF."

IT WAS THREE O'CLOCK IN THE MORNING, FOR GOD'S SAKE!

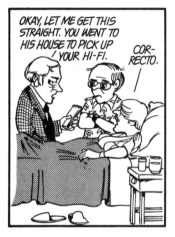

OKAY, LET ME GET THIS STRAIGHT. YOU WENT TO HIS HOUSE TO PICK UP YOUR HI-FI.

CORRECTO.

YOU'RE WALKING THROUGH THE DEN WHEN YOU SEE DUKE UP ON THE LANDING. WITHOUT WARNING, HE JUST EMPTIES A HANDGUN AT YOU.

STRANGE BUT TRUE.

MAY I ASK WHY YOU DID THAT?

I'M CAUTIOUS BY NATURE. I DON'T LIKE TO WALK INTO A DARK ROOM UNTIL I'VE SOFTENED IT UP.

DO YOU REALIZE THAT'S COMPLETELY INSANE?

IT IS?

DON'T RULE IT OUT, DUKE. IT'S A GOOD DEFENSE.

LOOK, I'M TELLING YOU, IT WAS ALL JUST A TERRIBLE ACCIDENT! I THOUGHT HE WAS A RACCOON, FOR GOD'S SAKE!

MAYBE. BUT I'M GOING TO HAVE TO TAKE YOU DOWNTOWN ANYWAY.

NOW SEE WHAT YOU'VE DONE!

YOU TRIED TO KILL ME, MAN.

LOOK, O'MALLEY, LET'S BE REASONABLE. DON'T YOU HAVE SOME FAVORITE CHARITY?

NOW HE'S TRYING TO BRIBE YOU!

ARE YOU TRYING TO BRIBE ME?

NOT IF YOU'RE GOING TO GET SNITTY ABOUT IT.

OFFICER, DO YOUR DUTY!

OKAY, LET'S HAVE YOUR HOME ADDRESS FIRST..

LOOK, LIEUTENANT, LET'S BE REASONABLE, OKAY?

A REPUTATION IS AT STAKE HERE! LIKE YOURSELF, I'M A LIFE-LONG PUBLIC SERVANT! IN FACT, I'M JUST ABOUT TO RUN FOR POLITICAL OFFICE..

POLITICAL OFFICE? NO KIDDING?

THAT WOULD EXPLAIN ALL THE CAMERAS OUTSIDE.

OH, NO..

GOOD EVENING. TODAY THE GOVERNORS OF FOUR NEW ENGLAND STATES ASKED FOR EMERGENCY FEDERAL AID TO HELP CONTROL GROWING INFESTATIONS OF THE AMERICAN PREPPY.

CITING THE THREAT OF QUARANTINE FROM NEIGHBORING STATES, THE FOUR GOVERNORS ANNOUNCED A JOINT PROGRAM TO COMBAT WHAT IS BEING REGARDED AS A PARTICULARLY VIRULENT STRAIN OF WASP.

GOVERNOR KING OF MASSACHUSETTS, WHOSE STATE IS HARDEST HIT, BLAMED THE NEW POLITICAL CLIMATE IN WASHINGTON FOR THE PROLIFERATION OF THESE PESKY ELITISTS.

AERIAL SPRAYING IS EXPECTED TO COMMENCE AT ONCE.

GOOD EVENING. TODAY IN WASHINGTON, A STORM OF CONTROVERSY WAS UNLEASHED BY THE NEWS THAT FOUR NEW ENGLAND GOVERNORS HAD DECIDED TO SPRAY LOCAL INFESTATIONS OF PREPPIES.

FUMED PREPPY STANDARD-BEARER GEORGE BUSH, "IT'S OUTRAGEOUS! THERE AREN'T EVEN THAT MANY PREPS IN NEW ENGLAND DURING THE OFF-SEASON. MOST OF US TIP WELL AND LEAVE BY LABOR DAY."

MEANWHILE, THE CAUSES OF THE PREP EXPLOSION ARE STILL UNDER INVESTIGATION, BUT PRELIMINARY FINDINGS SUGGEST THAT THE REAGANS' INFATUATION WITH THE WEALTHY AND SOCIALLY CONNECTED IS A MAJOR FACTOR.

WHITE HOUSE SPOKESWOMAN MUFFY BRANDON DISMISSED SUCH SPECULATION AS TACKY.

"..AND THE GOVERNOR NOTED THAT LIMITED AERIAL SPRAYING OVER PREPPY BREEDING GROUNDS LIKE GREENWICH, CONNECTICUT, HAD ONLY SERVED TO RAISE PROPERTY VALUES IN NEARBY WESTPORT."

BOY.. I HAD NO IDEA THE PREPPY PROBLEM HAD GOTTEN SO OUT OF HAND..

THE GOVERNOR'S DOING THE RIGHT THING. STATEWIDE SPRAYING IS THE ONLY SOLUTION.

"OTHER PROPOSALS, SUCH AS REFORMING THE INHERITANCE TAX LAWS OR SHUTTING DOWN SELECTED BOARDING SCHOOLS, WERE REJECTED AS TOO LIMITED TO IMPACT ON PREPPY POPULATIONS."

"STERILIZING MALE PREPS WAS ALSO VIEWED AS UNACCEPTABLE."

WHY?

TOO EXPENSIVE. THEY'D ALL WANT SPECIALISTS.

WE'RE BACK! I'M TALKING BY PHONE TO MR. LARRY CLEAVER, HEAD OF CONNECTICUT'S CONTROVERSIAL NEW PREPPY ERADICATION PROGRAM..

MR. CLEAVER, ASIDE FROM AERIAL SPRAYING, WILL YOU BE TAKING OTHER MEASURES TO CONTROL PREP POPULATIONS?

OH, MOST DEFINITELY, MARK..

WHAT WE'RE TRYING TO DO IS GET THE AVERAGE CITIZEN INVOLVED. TO THIS END, THE STATE WILL BE GRANTING TAX CREDITS TO ANYONE WHO TURNS IN SIX OR MORE ALLIGATOR SHIRTS.

PREPPY PELTS, AS IT WERE.

RIGHT. HOW HE GETS 'EM IS HIS BUSINESS.

MR. CLEAVER, I'M SURE MANY PEOPLE ARE WONDERING RIGHT NOW IF THERE ISN'T SOME LESS RADICAL WAY OF CONTROLLING THE SPREAD OF PREPPIES THAN AERIAL SPRAYING..

FOR INSTANCE, HAVE YOU CONSIDERED DISRUPTING THE REPRODUCTIVE CYCLE OF ADULT PREPPIES?

YES, BUT THE PROBLEM THERE IS THAT PREPPIES MATE SO RARELY, AND THEN ONLY ON THE ADVICE OF THEIR FAMILY ATTORNEYS.

HOW ABOUT CROSS-BREEDING THEM WITH HIGH SCHOOL GRADUATES?

WELL, WE'RE TRYING TO AVOID THAT KIND OF SOCIAL ENGINEERING.

VICE-PRESIDENT BUSH, DO YOU THINK THE NEW ESTATE LAWS HAVE CONTRIBUTED TO THE CURRENT PREP EXPLOSION?

GOSH, I DON'T THINK SO. IN WHAT WAY?

WELL, SIR, WHEN OLD PREPS DIE OFF, THE NEW TAX LAWS NOW ALLOW BABY PREPPIES TO RETAIN THEIR FAMILY FORTUNES INTACT. ISN'T THIS JUST ONE MORE BREAK FOR THE WELL-HEELED?

LADIES AND GENTLEMEN, I HAVE ONLY ONE THING TO SAY TO YOU ON THE SUBJECT: THE GREATEST PREP OF THEM ALL, F. SCOTT FITZGERALD, DIED VIRTUALLY PENNILESS.

UM.. YOUR POINT BEING, SIR?

NEVER AGAIN.

MR. SLACKMEYER, I'M SURE YOU AND YOUR COLLEAGUES ON THE COUNCIL OF ECONOMIC ADVISORS ARE AWARE OF THE HIGHLY UNFAVORABLE MARKET RESPONSE TO REAGANOMICS..

OF COURSE, SIR.

AS A RECENT LEADER OF THE FINANCIAL COMMUNITY YOURSELF, CAN YOU THINK OF ANY REASON WHY WALL STREET SHOULD BE REACTING SO NEGATIVELY TO YOUR CURRENT POLICIES?

WELL, SENATOR, AS HARD AS IT IS FOR ME TO ACCEPT THE POSSIBILITY, I'M AFRAID WALL STREET'S HOSTILITY MAY BE .. WELL, PERSONAL.

PERSONAL, MR. SLACKMEYER?

LET'S JUST SAY I HAD A FEW HEADS BROUGHT TO ME IN MY DAY, SENATOR.

SENATOR, WHAT WE'RE SEEING NOW IS **RAMPANT** OPPORTUNISM! INVESTORS ARE TAKING ADVANTAGE OF HIGH INTEREST RATES TO SCORE BIG IN THE MONEY FUNDS!

IT'S A MARKET OF SHAME NOW, SENATOR. HELL, I DON'T **KNOW** THE PLACE ANYMORE! THE WALL STREET I KNEW WAS VIBRANT, VISIONARY, GUTSY, NOT NERVOUS, GREEDY AND SHORT-SIGHTED!

I'M **ASHAMED** TO HAVE EVER BEEN A FINANCIER! THESE PEOPLE DON'T CARE IF THE PRESIDENT'S PLAN SUCCEEDS! ALL WALL STREET'S INTERESTED IN IS **MAKING MONEY!**

UM.. WHICH IS, OF COURSE, ONE OF ITS NATURAL FUNCTIONS.

MANFULLY CONCEDED, SIR!

YES?

MR. SLACKMEYER, WALL STREET IS CALLING ON LINE TWO.

WALL STREET? HOW CAN AN ENTIRE COMMUNITY OF INVESTORS BE ON THE LINE?

WELL, SIR, WHILE IT'S TRUE THE MARKET IS MADE UP OF MANY ELEMENTS, THEY GENERALLY SPEAK WITH ONE VOICE.

WELL.. OKAY, I'LL TAKE THE CALL.

YES, SIR.

WALL STREET! HOW ARE YOU, OLD BOY?

NERVOUS. JITTERY. OUT OF SORTS.

SO WHAT'S YOUR BEEF NOW, WALL STREET?

WELL, WASHINGTON, WE'RE A LITTLE MIFFED YOU'RE STILL TRYING TO PIN YOUR PROBLEMS ON US.

WELL, WALL STREET, WE JUST CAN'T FIGURE YOU OUT! HERE YOU HAVE THE MOST SYMPATHETIC ADMINISTRATION IN DECADES AND YOU'RE KILLING US!

SORRY, WASHINGTON, WE'RE NOT BUYING THAT. WE RESPOND TO ECONOMIC REALITIES, NOT POLITICAL NEEDS. IF THE TWO OVERLAP, GREAT. IF THEY DON'T, YOU'RE ON YOUR OWN.

YOU'RE ALL HEART, WALL STREET.

HEY, AT LEAST WE DON'T CALL KETCHUP A VEGETABLE.

PETITION? WHAT PETITION, THAD?

YOU HAVEN'T HEARD? THE SIERRA CLUB IS ORGANIZING A PETITION DEMANDING WATT'S REMOVAL. I THOUGHT WE MIGHT JOIN FORCES.

WHAT A **GREAT** IDEA, THADIUS! HOW MANY SIGNATURES DO THEY EXPECT TO GET?

OVER A MILLION. THEY'RE GOING TO PRESENT THE PETITION TO CONGRESS ON OCTOBER 19.

A MILLION.. WHY, THAT'S INCREDIBLE! IF WE START OUR OWN PETITION, I WONDER IF WE CAN GET ACCESS TO THEIR LIST..

WHAT FOR?

TO AVOID OVERLAPS, WE DON'T WANT TO DISCREDIT THEIR WHOLE DRIVE.

GOOD THOUGHT. IT'D BE JUST LIKE WATT TO CHECK.

FELLOW MEMBERS OF THE MARYLAND AUDUBON SOCIETY, I'M PLEASED TO REPORT TO THE BOARD THAT A SPLENDID OPPORTUNITY HAS PRESENTED ITSELF!

THE SIERRA CLUB HAS BEGUN A PETITION DRIVE CALLING FOR WATT'S REMOVAL. I PROPOSE WE JOIN THAT EFFORT AND CANVAS OUR OWN NEIGHBORHOOD!

YOU MEAN, ACTUALLY GO DOOR TO DOOR TO PEOPLE'S HOMES, DICK?

YES, IF I NEED BE.

WHY, I HAVEN'T DONE THAT SINCE BROWNIES!

WHAT IF THEY'RE IN THE MIDDLE OF DINNER?

YOU CAN ALWAYS GO BACK LATER, JEREMY.

BUT BY THEN, THEY'LL BE WATCHING T.V.!

JEREMY'S RIGHT, DICK. IT COULD GET STICKY.

GB Trudeau

..AND I BELIEVE A PETITION DRIVE WOULD SHOW THE SKEPTICS JUST HOW SERIOUS WE ARE!

WHAT WOULD OUR PITCH BE, DICK?

OUR MESSAGE WOULD BE THAT WATT'S PRO-DEVELOPMENT VIEWS THREATEN THE CONSERVATION GOALS SUPPORTED BY MOST AMERICANS. FOR THAT REASON, WE'RE DEMANDING HIS REMOVAL!

IF THERE ARE NO OBJECTIONS, I MOVE WE HIT THE STREETS FIRST THING TOMORROW!

AN OUTING! HOW EXCITING!

WHAT ABOUT SHOES, DICK? WHAT'S BEST, RUBBER SOLES?

UH..RUBBER SOLES WOULD BE FINE, JEREMY.

I DON'T HAVE ANY. I CAN'T GO.

WHAT IF WE RUN INTO TEAR GAS, DICK? SHOULD WE MEET BACK HERE?

GBTrudeau

GOOD MORNING!

HEAVENS, DICK! WHERE ARE YOU OFF TO SO BRIGHT AND EARLY?

TO GARNER SIGNATURES FOR MY PETITION DRIVE! I THOUGHT I'D START DOWN AT THE CLUB.

THE CLUB? BUT IT'S BEDROCK CONSERVATIVE, DEAR. ISN'T THAT A WASTE OF TIME?

MAYBE, BUT EVEN IF I ONLY GET A FEW NAMES, THEY'LL CARRY A LOT OF WEIGHT. IT'S THAD'S IDEA. HE'S HANDLING ALL THE PRESS.

SOUNDS LIKE A GOOD STRATEGY!

SO WHAT'S THE REACTION TO OUR DRIVE UP ON THE HILL?

UM.. GUARDED, DEAR. SORT OF A WAIT AND SEE FEELING.

GBTrudeau

..AND THAT'S WHY I'M URGING YOU TO SIGN, BURBERRY— FOR THE GOOD OF THE WHOLE NATION!

THIS MAN WATT MUST BE STOPPED BEFORE HE CAN PUT ALL OUR PRECIOUS RESOURCES INTO THE HANDS OF OIL AND OTHER SPECIAL..

OH, DICK, DICK, OLD BOY..

WHAT?

DICK, WOULD YOU LIKE TO SEE THIS CLUB ACCEPTING ARABS ONE DAY? ARE YOU READY FOR THAT?

WELL, NO, OF COURSE NOT, BUT..

LOOK, DICK, IF IT'S TREES YOU WANT, JUST USE MY CAMP IN MAINE ANY TIME!

GBTrudeau

I REALIZE THIS WOULD BE HARD FOR YOU TO DO, TODD. YOU'VE ALWAYS BEEN A DIE-HARD REAGAN MAN AND I RESPECT THAT. BUT THIS FELLOW WATT MUST BE STOPPED!

WHAT DO YOU SAY, OLD BOY, WILL YOU SIGN MY PETITION? WE'VE KNOWN EACH OTHER EVER SINCE ANDOVER. WILL YOU DO IT FOR AN OLD SCHOOLCHUM?

WAITER!

SIR?

SHOW THIS TRAITOR TO HIS CLASS BACK TO HIS TABLE.

I'LL JUST LEAVE A COPY IN CASE YOU CHANGE YOUR MIND.

GBTrudeau

TRUMBULL! I'VE BEEN LOOKING EVERYWHERE FOR YOU, OLD BOY! WILL YOU SIGN MY PETITION?

WHAT PETITION IS THAT, DICK?

I'M PETITIONING CONGRESS TO IMMEDIATELY DISMISS JAMES WATT FOR GROSS DERELICTION OF HIS DUTIES AS STEWARD OF AMERICA'S NATURAL RESOURCES!

HEE, HEE! YEAH, OKAY, I'LL HELP YOU OUT..

SPLENDID!

WHAT IS THIS REALLY, DICK, THE TOURNAMENT SIGN-UP SHEET?

HOW'D YOU MAKE OUT AT THE CLUB WITH YOUR PETITION, DEAR?

NOT HALF BAD. I GOT NEARLY 15 SIGNATURES.

WONDERFUL! DID DEAR TODD SMITHSON COME THROUGH?

NO, TODD WOULDN'T SIGN. HE'S GOT TOO MUCH MONEY TIED UP IN ENERGY STOCKS NOW.

OH..WELL, HOW ABOUT JOCK TRIPLER ..OR EDDIE WHITE?

NO. JOCK GAVE MONEY TO REAGAN'S CAMPAIGN, AND EDDIE REPRESENTS MOBIL.

THEN WHO **ARE** ALL THESE PEOPLE, DEAR?

THE CADDIES.

FELLOW BIRDER!

YES? WHO CALLS?

RICHARD DAVENPORT FROM THE AUDUBON SOCIETY! WOULD YOU SIGN OUR PETITION DEMANDING JAMES WATT'S DISMISSAL?

SURE, I'M GAME. GIVE IT HERE. GLAD TO HELP.

ANY OTHER BIRDERS OUT THERE?

WELL, A COUPLE OF FELLAHS WENT OUT TO MILLER'S POINT LOOKIN' FOR A PINTAIL DUCK.

HOW LONG AGO WAS THAT?

YEARS AGO. BEFORE THE WAR. FRIENDS OF YOURS?

DUKE! WHAT?.. HOW?..

I TOLD YOUR GUARD HE HAD A PHONE CALL. BRIGHT FELLOW.

DUKE.. PLEASE.. LET'S BE REASONABLE!

LISTEN VERY CAREFULLY, DOG-BREATH. YOU'RE GOING TO PICK UP THAT PHONE AND CALL THE POLICE.

SURE, DUKE. WHAT FOR?

YOU'RE GOING TO TELL THAT DETECTIVE YOU'VE DECIDED TO DROP ALL CHARGES. AND YOU'RE GOING TO TELL IT TO HIM VERY CALMLY.

CALMLY, YOU SAY.

RIGHT. YOU'RE EVEN GOING TO THROW IN A JOKE OR TWO.

"10:00, UNIVERSITY AWARD CEREMONY; 11:30, TRUSTEES MEETING; 1:30, FACULTY MEETING; 4:00, ALUMNI ASSOCIATION; 6:30, STUDENT RADIO INTERVIEW.." MY GOD, WHAT A DAY!

ONCE AGAIN, I GET TO SPEND MY EVERY WAKING HOUR WITH BORING OLD GRADS, BELLIGERENT TEACHERS, ARROGANT KIDS..

OH, STOP WHINING, FOR PETE'S SAKE!

AM I SUPPOSED TO FEEL SORRY FOR YOU BECAUSE YOU'RE A COLLEGE PRESIDENT? GIVE ME A BREAK! YOU OUGHTA TRY BEING A SECRETARY!

..SURLY UNDER-LINGS..

I'M SICK TO **DEATH** OF HEARING HOW TOUGH LIFE IS AT THE TOP! !

IT IS A SPECIAL HONOR FOR ME TO PRE-SENT THE UNIVERSITY MEDAL TODAY TO GEORGE P. CONGDON, III. IN EVERY RE-SPECT, HE IS A MOST WORTHY RECIPIENT..

THIS I GOTTA HEAR!

TO GEORGE CONGDON, THIS UNIVERSITY AND THIS PRESIDENT HAVE OFTEN TURNED FOR COUNSEL, INSPIRATION, LEADERSHIP..

..AND A NEW FIELD HOUSE!

SERIOUSLY, GEORGE HAS SOME-THING EVERY UNIVERSITY LOOKS FOR IN A LOYAL ALUMNUS..

EIGHT MILLION BUCKS AND A BAD HEART!

HA! HA! HA! HA! HA! HA! HA! HA! HA!

HA! HA! HA! HA! HA!

GEORGE, IT'D BE NICE IF WE COULD GET THROUGH THIS WITH SOME DIGNITY.

SORRY, BIG GUY. CARRY ON!

HA! HA!

.. AND I'M PLEASED TO REPORT TO THE TRUSTEES THAT THANKS TO OUR NEW COST-CUTTING MEASURES, THE UNIVERSITY IS FINALLY BACK ON SOLID FINANCIAL GROUND!

THERE IS AS WELL A NEW ACADEMIC PROSPERITY. RIGOROUS CURRICULUM RE-QUIREMENTS HAVE BEEN REINSTATED. TEACH-ERS ARE TEACHING, STUDENTS ARE STUDY-ING, LIBRARIES ARE FILLED TO CAPACITY!

IN SHORT, LADIES AND GENTLEMEN, A MOST GRATIFYING PICTURE. I'D BE HAPPY TO ENTERTAIN ANY QUESTIONS YOU MIGHT HAVE NOW.

YEAH, KING, HOW COME THE TEAM'S BEEN PLAYING LIKE A BUNCH OF SICK NUNS?

I'LL HAVE TO GET BACK TO YOU ON THAT, PHIL.

.. AND I'M HAPPY TO REPORT TO THE FACULTY THAT YOUR PROPOSALS HAVING TO DO WITH SALARY INCREASES, TENURE, AND PROMOTIONS WERE GIVEN THE MOST CAREFUL CONSIDERATION BY THE TRUSTEES!

THE BOARD ALSO SHARED YOUR CONCERN ABOUT THE DEVALUATION OF OUR GRADING SYSTEM, STEMMING FROM STUDENT PRESSURE ON TEACHERS NOT TO GIVE LOW MARKS WHICH MAY ADVERSELY AFFECT CAREER PROSPECTS..

HOWEVER, YOUR RECOMMENDATION OF A QUOTA SYSTEM FOR LETTER GRADES DID NOT STRIKE US AS A TERRIBLY PRACTICAL, NOT TO SAY EQUITABLE, SOLUTION TO THE PROBLEM.

HOW ABOUT OUR PROPOSAL TO ABOLISH "A's"?

IT WAS FELT THAT MIGHT BE A BIT DEMORALIZING FOR THE STUDENTS.

GENTLEMEN, THE TWO OF YOU HAVE DONE NOTHING BUT EMBARRASS ME WITH YOUR SQUABBLING OVER THE NUCLEAR WARNING SHOT..

"BONZO GOES TO WAR"
SCENE 82 TAKE 1

I WANT THIS SETTLED ONCE AND FOR ALL! DOES NATO HAVE A DEMONSTRATION BLAST SCENARIO OR NOT? CASPAR?

ABSOLUTELY NOT, SIR. IN FACT, WE MAY NOT EVEN HAVE THE CAPABILITY.

GIVEN THE DELICACY OF THIS KIND OF DEPLOYMENT, THE TECHNICAL ASPECTS ARE VERY WORRISOME. FRANKLY, I'M NOT PERSUADED WE COULD DELIVER SUCH A WEAPON ON TIME AND ON TARGET.

HMM.. WHAT DO YOU THINK, AL?

MR. PRESIDENT, I LIKE TO THINK HIROSHIMA SPEAKS FOR ITSELF.

SO HOW'S THE REACTION BEEN TO OUR NEW PEACE INITIATIVE, ED?

WELL, SIR, I'M AFRAID IT'S STARTING TO BE SEEN AS A LITTLE CYNICAL..

"SALT IN THE WOUND"
SCENE 7 TAKE 1

CYNICAL? HOW COME?

BECAUSE WE PROPOSED A PLAN BASED ON MISSILE COUNTS WE KNEW TO BE TOTALLY UNACCEPTABLE TO THE SOVIETS.

AS A RESULT, IT LOOKED LIKE YOU WERE MORE INTERESTED IN SCORING A PUBLIC RELATIONS COUP IN EUROPE THAN IN TAKING ANY REAL STEPS TO REDUCE THE THREAT OF NUCLEAR WAR.

HEY, C'MON, I RENAMED SALT, DIDN'T I?

WELL, YES, SIR, BUT THAT ONLY MEANT YOU WERE COMMITTED TO CHANGING THE STATIONERY.

ED, WHAT ARE YOU GETTING FROM CONGRESS ABOUT STOCKMAN? HAS HIS CREDIBILITY BEEN IRRETRIEVABLY COMPROMISED?

"DEATH OF A SALESMAN"
SCENE 21 TAKE 13

WELL, WE SHOULD FIND OUT TODAY. HE WENT UP TO THE HILL TODAY TO PRESENT OUR LATEST BUDGET DEFICIT FIGURES.

GOOD FOR HIM. THAT TAKES GUTS. I'M SURE THE COMMITTEE WILL RESPECT HIM FOR IT.

HA, HA! HA! HA! HA! HA! HA! HA!

NO? OKAY, HOW ABOUT $81 BILLION?

DON'T YOU THINK WE SHOULD GET UP, DEAR? IT'S NEARLY 9:30..

I KNOW.. I'VE JUST BEEN THINKING ABOUT DAVE STOCKMAN..

"CONGRESS MAKES AN OFFER"
SCENE 9 TAKE 107

WILL YOU HAVE TO LET HIM GO, DEAR?

NOPE. I'M NOT GIVING IN. AS I TOLD SENATOR BAKER YESTERDAY, CONGRESS CAN LEAN ON ME ALL THEY WANT, BUT DAVID STOCKMAN IS MY.. HEY!

WHAT'S WRONG, DEAR?

WHAT'S.. WHAT'S THAT DOWN AT THE FOOT OF THE BED?..

IT'S.. AIEE!

OH, MY GOD.. THE HEAD OF A TROJAN HORSE!

AS MUCH AS I HATE TO ADMIT IT, HOWARD'S RIGHT: OUR BIGGEST PROBLEM IS OTHER WOMEN. MANY WOMEN FEEL THAT ERA REPRESENTS A THREAT TO FAMILY LIFE AND THE TRADITIONAL MARRIAGE.

ERA HAS PUT THEM ON THE DEFENSIVE, MADE THEM FEEL INSECURE ABOUT HOMEMAKING.

I KNOW WHAT YOU MEAN. MY MOM USED TO SAY SHE WAS A HOUSEWIFE. NOW SHE SAYS SHE'S JUST A HOUSEWIFE.

THAT'S A VERY ASTUTE OBSERVATION, JEANIE. THE PROBLEM THEN BECOMES, HOW DO WE FEMINISTS REACH SUCH A WOMAN?

THROUGH COUPONS. HOUSEWIVES LOVE TO READ COUPONS!

ANY OTHER SUGGESTIONS?

I SUPPOSE I COULD JUST LEAVE HER A NOTE.

SORRY TO INTERRUPT, BUT I GOTTA GO TO THE BOYS' ROOM..

AGAIN? THAT'S THE THIRD TIME THIS MORNING, HOWARD!

YEAH, I KNOW, BUT I LIKE IT THERE. IT'S A GREAT PLACE TO BE WITH THE GUYS, YOU KNOW, TO TALK SPORTS, SING IN THE STALLS, PITCH PENNIES, TO JUST GET AWAY FROM IT ALL! SEE YOU ALL LATER.

GOSH..THE BOYS' ROOM SOUNDS LIKE A LOT OF FUN..

SAY, ELLIE, IF ERA IS PASSED, CAN WE..

NO, JEANIE! NO! NO! NO!

SIMPSON, THESE PROJECTIONS ARE STAGGERING! ARE YOU SURE YOU'VE GOT YOUR NUMBERS RIGHT?

I RAN THE FIGURES THROUGH THE COMPUTER TWICE, CHIEF.

SO WHAT ARE YOU RECOMMENDING? IF WE DON'T GET THIS DEFICIT UNDER CONTROL, THE TRUSTEES WILL HAVE MY HEAD!

WELL, SIR, THE LOGICAL PLACE TO START IS SALARIES.

GOOD! I CONCUR! IT'S TIME WE CUT A LITTLE OF THE FAT OUT OF THE FACULTY PAYROLL!

NOT TO MENTION ADMINISTRATION SALARIES.

I SAID FAT, SIMPSON, NOT BONE MARROW!

QUITE RIGHT, SIR. WE'VE SUFFERED ENOUGH.

..AND IF WE MAKE A 15% CUT ACROSS THE BOARD FOR ALL DEPARTMENTS..

WE'D HAVE AN OPEN REVOLT ON OUR HANDS.

THERE'S GOT TO BE A DIFFERENT WAY, SIMPSON. I DON'T THINK WE CAN AFFORD TO ANTAGONIZE SO MANY PEOPLE AT THE SAME TIME..

WELL, SIR, WE COULD ALWAYS MAKE JUST ONE MAJOR CUT..

WHAT DO YOU HAVE IN MIND, SIMPSON?

HOW STRONGLY DO YOU FEEL ABOUT THE SOCIOLOGY DEPARTMENT?

I DUNNO. IS IT ANY GOOD?

KNOW WHAT I'D BE DOING RIGHT NOW IF I WERE STILL IN GOVERNMENT, JIM?

NO, WHAT, PHIL?

I'D BE PUTTING IN ANOTHER 14-HOUR DAY AT A JOB LARGELY DEFINED BY MIND-NUMBING PAPERWORK, PETTY BUREAUCRATIC INFIGHTING AND INSULTING WAGES!

INSTEAD, I'M ENTERTAINING A DOZEN WEALTHY CLIENTS WITH CHAMPAGNE AND SIRLOIN IN A PRIVATE BOX AT THE SUPER-BOWL, AND ALL OF IT TAX-DEDUCTIBLE!

WELCOME BACK, BIG GUY!

GOD, I LOVE THE PRIVATE SECTOR!

TODAY "TIME" MAGAZINE PUBLISHED ITS SIXTH LENGTHY EXCERPT FROM THE CONTINUING MEMOIRS OF HENRY KISSINGER. THIS YEAR'S INSTALLMENTS ARE FROM THE LATEST KISSINGER VOLUME, "YEARS OF WHITEWASH," ALSO PUBLISHED BY "TIME."

MEET HENRY GRUNWALD, EDITOR OF "TIME." MR. GRUNWALD, ISN'T YOUR MAGAZINE'S FASCINATION WITH KISSINGER BEGINNING TO TURN INTO AN OBSESSION?

NO, I THINK IT'S SOMETHING RATHER MORE SPECIAL.

MY EDITORS AND I HAVE BECOME THE KEEPERS OF THE KISSINGER FLAME. WE DOTE ON HIM, WE CONSULT HIM, WE WORSHIPFULLY TRACK HIS EVERY MOVE. HIS VIEW OF HISTORY, TO WHICH WE HOLD ALL THE RIGHTS, IS GOSPEL—UNEXAMINED AND IMMACULATE.

I SEE. SO IT'S MORE LIKE AN ORGANIZED RELIGION.

RIGHT. IN FACT, WE'RE APPLYING FOR TAX-EXEMPT STATUS.

THE KISSINGER CULT AT "TIME" MAGAZINE—IS IT A MENACE?

WHO CARES? ENOUGH ON KISSINGER, ALREADY!

I HEAR HIS LATEST MEMOIR IS OVER 1500 PAGES, AND HE'S STILL ONLY UP TO 1975!

WELL, THE GOOD DOCTOR HAS MUCH TO ANSWER FOR, MICHAEL.

POOR HENRY! WHAT A TIME TO BE BEDRIDDEN! HE'S MISSING ALL THE EXCITEMENT.

NOT TO WORRY. I'M SURE HE'S EXPERIENCING NO SHORTAGE OF WELL-WISHERS.

HI, DOC! HOW'S OUR FAVORITE COVER-BOY?

NURSE!

WE'RE ALL SO RELIEVED THE OPERATION WAS A SUCCESS, DOC. THE WHOLE CLASS WAS WORRIED SICK ABOUT YOU!

I CAN IMAGINE, MR. WEINBURGER.

SO WHAT WAS IT LIKE BEING TOLD YOU NEEDED A TRIPLE-BYPASS, SIR? DID YOUR WHOLE LIFE FLASH BEFORE YOUR EYES?

NO. ONLY 1968 TO 1975. THE HISTORIC YEARS.

JEEPERS. HOW LONG DID THAT TAKE?

ABOUT A WEEK.

WOW..

INCLUDING REVISIONS?

IT'S TOO BAD YOU'VE BEEN UNDER THE WEATHER, PROFESSOR KISSINGER. YOU'RE MISSING ALL THE HULLABALOO OVER YOUR NEW BOOK!

DON'T WORRY, MR. PERKINS. MY OFFICE KEEPS IN TOUCH.

IT'S A GREAT BOOK, SIR. MOST OF THE CLASS IS WAITING TO BUY IT IN PAPERBACK, BUT I COULDN'T WAIT!

YOU'VE READ IT, ALREADY?

EVERY WORD, SIR! IT'S ENTHRALLING! I'M KIND OF A MEMOIRS BUFF, AND I THINK YOURS IS ONE OF THE BEST I'VE EVER READ!

WHY, THANK YOU, PERKINS, I..

HAVE YOU SEEN EDDIE FISHER'S YET? THAT'S ANOTHER GREAT ONE!

EASY, BARNEY, THEY'RE COMPETITORS.

GET WELL SOON, DOC! ALL YOUR ENEMIES MISS YOU!

SOME PEOPLE JUST WON'T LET OLD WOUNDS HEAL, EH, MR. KISSINGER?

YOU MIGHT SAY THAT.

WELL, I CAN SYMPATHIZE WITH THEIR FEELINGS. WHEN I HELPED CRACK YOUR CHEST LAST MONTH, I MYSELF STARTED THINKING ABOUT MY DAYS IN THE ANTI-WAR MOVEMENT..

IT WAS AN AMAZING MOMENT. AS WE FINISHED UP THE THIRD BYPASS, IT SUDDENLY HIT ME THAT I WAS HOLDING THE HEART OF A MAN WHOSE POLICIES HAD ONCE CONDEMNED THOUSANDS TO DEATH!

THEN I THOUGHT OF MY HIPPOCRATIC OATH AND SEWED YOU UP.

GOOD OATH, THAT.

BECAUSE YOU ASKED FOR IT, CAMPERS, BACK WITH US TODAY IS TOP POP DOC, DAN ASHER, HERE TO PLUG HIS LATEST, "THE MELLOW PARENT: SHARING YOUR SPACE WITH DEPENDENTS." SO WHAT'S THE POOP ON THE BOOK, DANIEL?

WELL, MARK, EVERYONE SEEMS TO BE INTO CHILD-REARING THESE DAYS, SO I JUST FLASHED ON A NEED FOR A NEW PARENTING HOW-TO. IT'S ALL IN THERE—EVERYTHING FROM HIRING YOUR FIRST NANNY TO NON-SEXIST CONDITIONING TO WHERE TO HIDE YOUR DOPE!

AND YOU BRING A WEALTH OF EXPERIENCE TO YOUR ADVICE, DON'T YOU, DAN?

I SURE DO. I'VE GOT TWO KIDS FROM MY FIRST MARRIAGE, ONE FROM MY SECOND, AND TWO GREAT STEP-KIDS FROM MY THIRD.

SO THERE'S A LOT OF LAUGHTER AROUND THE ASHER HOUSEHOLD, EH?

ACTUALLY, ONLY ON WEEKENDS. BUT MY LAWYER'S WORKING ON IT.

WE'RE BACK AND RAPPING WITH DR. DAN ASHER, WHO HAS JUST SKYED IN FROM THE COAST TO HYPE HIS LATEST POP EPIC, "THE MELLOW PARENT: SHARING YOUR SPACE WITH DEPENDENTS."

LET'S TAKE IT FROM THE TOP, DOCTOR. WHAT'S YOUR ADVICE TO THE MELLOW MOTHER-TO-BE?

WELL, BASICALLY, IT'S TO GET IN TOUCH WITH YOUR BODY. MORNING SICKNESS, CRAMPS, ACHING BACK—JUST LET IT ALL HAPPEN!

ON THE BIG DAY ITSELF, GO ORGANIC. ANIMALS DON'T USE DRUGS, NEITHER SHOULD YOU. THE BIRTHING PROCESS IS BOTH VIOLENT AND BEAUTIFUL. GET INTO THE PAIN—EXPERIENCE IT FULLY!

AND YOUR ADVICE TO THE MELLOW HUBBY?

TAKE THE DAY OFF. SHOW SOME CLASS.

DR. DAN, IN YOUR PREFACE TO "THE MELLOW PARENT", YOU MAKE THE POINT THAT THE BIGGEST DECISION A COUPLE WILL EVER FACE IS **WHEN** TO BECOME PARENTS, RIGHT?

THAT'S RIGHT, MARK. TIMING IS THE HOT SUBJECT TODAY, ESPECIALLY TO WOMEN OVER 30. MANY OF THEM ARE TRYING TO BUILD CAREERS, BUT THEY HEAR THEIR BIOLOGICAL CLOCKS TICKING AWAY.

THE MELLOW HUBBY SHOULD COMPENSATE BY BEING CIRCUMSPECT. EVEN IF HE INTENDS TO PARTICIPATE FULLY, HE SHOULD MAKE SURE HIS WIFE IS **UP** TO BOTH RAISING A KID AND BRINGING HOME THAT CRITICAL SECOND INCOME!

BUT HOW CAN HE TELL IN ADVANCE?

START HER OUT ON A PUPPY. SEE HOW MUCH IT EATS INTO HER TIME.

DAN, ONE OF THE MOST FASCINATING CHAPTERS OF YOUR BOOK IS ENTITLED "QUALITY TIME." I WONDER IF YOU COULD EXPLAIN THE QUALITY TIME CONCEPT TO US.

FOR SURE, MARK. QUALITY TIME IS THE KIND OF TIME YOU SPEND WITH YOUR KIDS IF YOU'RE REALLY TOO PRESSED TO GIVE THEM THE MORE TRADITIONAL QUANTITY TIME!

BY GIVING A CHILD QUALITY TIME, THAT IS, HIGHLY CONCENTRATED DOSAGES OF FOCUSED ATTENTION, THE BUSY PARENT CAN SHAVE VALUABLE HOURS OFF THE TIME REQUIRED TO IMPACT HIS CHILD'S DEVELOPMENT.

SO QUALITY TIME IS BASICALLY A TIME-SAVER.

RIGHT. IT WORKS WITH OLD PEOPLE, TOO, BY THE WAY.

DAN, IN YOUR BOOK YOU CLAIM THAT A MAJOR PROBLEM FOR THE MELLOW PARENT IS DESIGNER JEANS.

THAT'S RIGHT, MARK. DESIGNER JEANS ARE TEARING A LOT OF FAMILIES APART.

BECAUSE OF BROOKE SHIELDS AND ALL THE T.V. ADS, KIDS TODAY ARE CLAMORING FOR STATUS JEANS. UNFORTUNATELY, THEY GROW OUT OF THEM QUICKLY, SO MANY PARENTS DON'T THINK THEY'RE WORTH THE MONEY.

SO WHICH SIDE OF THE ISSUE DO YOU COME DOWN ON, DAN?

I'M PRO-JEANS, MARK. KIDS WILL BE JUDGED ON THEIR JEANS ALL THEIR LIVES. PARENTS WHO SKIMP ON JEANS GIVE THEIR CHILDREN A SOCIAL HANDICAP!

HOW ABOUT DESIGNER WATER? SAME THING?

ABSOLUTELY. THE KID WHO DOESN'T HAVE PERRIER IN HIS LUNCHPAIL COULD MISS THE BOAT!

HEY, ALPHONSE, WHERE'S THE MAN?

HE'S OUT AT SEA, MR. RODRIGUEZ. HE LEFT THREE DAYS AGO.

WHEN'S HE DUE BACK? I GOT A JOB FOR HIM.

SORRY, SIR, MR. DUKE TOLD ME NOT TO ACCEPT ANY NEW BUSINESS FOR HIM. HE'S GOING TO BE GONE AT LEAST FIVE WEEKS.

FIVE **WEEKS?** WHERE'S HE GOING, COLOMBIA?

NO, SIR, THE FALKLAND ISLANDS. HE'S TAKING A CHARTER OF SIGHTSEERS DOWN TO WATCH THE BRITISH BLOCKADE.

♫ DON'T CRY FOR ME, **AR**-GENTINA! ♫

HA! HA!

EXCUSE ME, SIR. WE'RE OUT OF ICE.

DAMN! WE HAVEN'T EVEN REACHED CUBA YET!

• THE ICE QUEEN COMETH •

HI, TED. A LITTLE CHILLY OUT HERE. WHY DON'T YOU COME BACK IN?

NO WAY, RICK. NOT UNTIL SHE AGREES TO LET US DO OUR JOB.

I WON'T WATCH 11 YEARS OF WORK GO DOWN THE DRAIN. THE EPA WAS ONE OF THE FEW AGENCIES IN TOWN WHICH WERE REALLY MAKING A DIFFERENCE!

SEE THOSE CARS DOWN THERE, RICK? WHY, THE AIR'S SO CLEAR NOW YOU CAN READ THEIR LICENSE PLATES FROM HERE!

WOW.. THAT'S AMAZING..

A FEW YEARS AGO, YOU COULDN'T EVEN SEE THE STREET!

OKAY, SIMPSON, YOU WIN. I'LL REINSTATE THE ENFORCEMENT DIVISION.

WILL YOU LET US PROSECUTE POLLUTION VIOLATORS AS WE SEE FIT?

UNTIL SUCH TIME AS THE PRESIDENT CAN GUT THE LAWS, YES.

DO YOU PROMISE?

I PROMISE.

OKAY, I'M COMING IN.

I LIED. YOU'RE FIRED.

AARRGH!

QUICK, SHUT THE WINDOW!

HI, BERNIE! WHAT ARE YOU DOING HERE?

PROFESSOR CAVENDISH IS OUT SICK TODAY. BERNIE'S FILLING IN FOR HIM.

BUT THIS IS INTRO COMPUTER SCIENCE! AREN'T YOU KIND OF SLUMMING, BERNIE?

I DON'T MIND. I'VE PLANNED SOMETHING SPECIAL FOR YOU TODAY— COMPUTER GENERATED WAR GAMES!

WAR GAMES?

I'VE WORKED UP A PROGRAM TO SIMULATE A NUCLEAR CONFRONTATION. EACH OF YOU GETS TO PLAY SOMEONE IN THE COMMAND CHAIN.

I WANT TO BE AL HAIG!

I DIBS BUSH.

ONE AT A TIME, ONE AT A TIME.

CAN I BE THE MAD B-52 PILOT?

GOOD MORNING, ALL, AND WELCOME TO THE WALDEN WAR GAMES. FOR THE NEXT HOUR, WE WILL BE RESPONDING TO COMPUTER SCENARIOS SIMULATING A NUCLEAR CONFRONTATION. THE PROGRAM IS MODELLED AFTER SIMILAR EXERCISES STAGED BY THE PENTAGON.

EACH OF YOU HAS BEEN ASSIGNED A PLACE IN THE CHAIN OF COMMAND. AS THE CRISIS GROWS, YOU MUST USE YOUR CODE BOOKS TO RELAY ORDERS TO YOUR STRATEGIC FORCES.

IN APPROXIMATELY 15 SECONDS, THE PROGRAM WILL APPEAR ON YOUR DISPLAYS. IF AT ANY TIME, YOU WISH TO TRY TO RESOLVE THE CRISIS THROUGH QUIET DIPLOMACY, SIMPLY PRESS THE CLEAR BUTTON.

READY?.. LET THE GAMES BEGIN!

CODE RED! CODE..UH.. NEVER MIND. JUST A FLOCK OF GEESE.

LACEY, AS EXCITED AS I AM ABOUT THIS BABY, I'M ALSO SCARED TO DEATH. AFTER ALL, I REALLY SCREWED UP MY FIRST TIME.

YOU MEAN J.J.? WOULD THAT YOU "SCREW UP" HALF AS WELL THE SECOND TIME, DEAR!

BUT I WASN'T THERE! I RAN OUT! HOW DO I KNOW I WON'T DO IT AGAIN? AND WHAT ABOUT MY CAREER? CAN I HANDLE BOTH? IS IT FAIR TO DO BOTH? CAN I COUNT ON RICK TO DO HIS SHARE? GOD, I JUST DON'T KNOW!

GRAPPLE, GRAPPLE.

AT LEAST THIS TIME YOU KNOW THE QUESTIONS, DEAR.

YES, JOANIE?

A PRETTY HEAVY LETTER JUST ROLLED IN, BOSS.

WHAT'S IT SAY, DEAR?

"DEAR MRS. DAVENPORT: LAY OFF THE RAY DONOVAN INVESTIGATION, OR YOUSE COULD BE PUSHING DAISIES."

WHAT A STRANGE LETTER. I'M NOT EVEN ON ORRIN HATCH'S COMMITTEE!

WHICH SHOULDN'T BE TOO SURPRISING, SINCE YOU'RE ALSO NOT IN THE SENATE.

HOW IS HE SPELLING "YOUSE", DEAR?

JUST LIKE IT SOUNDS. MIND IF I LEAK THIS?

YEAH, LEMME SPEAK TO LACEY DAVENPORT.

THIS IS SHE.

LISTEN, LADY, YOUSE BETTER CALL OFF TH' COMMITTEE INVESTIGATION OF RAY DONOVAN, OR YOUSE AND YOURS GONNA BE SLEEPIN' WITH TH' FISHES!

I'M NOT ON THAT COMMITTEE, YOUNG MAN. THEY'RE SENATE HEARINGS, NOT HOUSE.

DEY ARE? GEE, I'M SORRY, I THOUGHT..

MOREOVER, IF YOU MUST MAKE THREATENING CALLS, YOU COULD AT LEAST BE COURTEOUS ENOUGH TO CALL AT A DECENT HOUR!

HEY, LADY, I SAID I WAS SORRY.

A LISTED PHONE NUMBER SHOULD NEVER BE ABUSED, YOUNG MAN!

HE REALLY THREATENED YOU OVER THE PHONE, LACEY?

THAT'S NOT THE WORST OF IT. HE HAD THE TEMERITY TO CALL AT 3:30 IN THE MORNING!

BUT WHY, LACEY? WHAT DO THESE THREATS MEAN?

WELL, I'D SAY EITHER MR. DONOVAN CONSORTS WITH UNDERWORLD TYPES, OR HE'S THE VICTIM OF THE MOST EXTRAORDINARY STRING OF COINCIDENCES SINCE FRANK SINATRA.

EXCUSE ME, LACEY. THESE FLOWERS JUST CAME FOR YOU..

GOODNESS! HOW LOVELY! WHAT'S THE CARD SAY, DEAR?

"WITH APOLOGIES FROM THE NEW JERSEY MOB."

OH, DEAR. I MUST HAVE MADE HIM FEEL TERRIBLE.

THADIUS! WHAT A NICE SURPRISE! TO WHAT DO WE OWE THE PLEASURE?

DIDN'T DICK TELL YOU? WE'RE GOING BIRDING ON MATAGORDA ISLAND!

WHAT FUN! BUT AREN'T YOU A LITTLE LATE? HAVEN'T ALL THE BIRDS MIGRATED BY NOW?

WELL, A LOT OF THEM HAVE, BUT WE'RE AFRAID IT'S OUR LAST CHANCE!

WATT'S GIVING PARTIAL CONTROL OF THE ISLAND TO THE TEXAS PARKS COMMISSION, WHICH IS SO PRO-DEVELOPMENT IT ONCE VOTED TO TURN A CRITICAL WARBLER HABITAT INTO AN 18-HOLE GOLF COURSE!

OH, DEAR. I BETTER GO GET DICK AT ONCE!

NOT THAT IT WASN'T A PRETTY TOUGH CALL.

HI, DICK. READY TO GO?

I'M AFRAID I HAVE SOME BAD NEWS, THAD. I CAN'T LEAVE. I'VE JUST LEARNED LACEY'S LIFE IS IN DANGER!

WHAT?

NOW, DICK, THAT'S NOTHING TO WORRY ABOUT. I CALLED BILL WEBSTER TODAY AND THE FBI IS CHECKING INTO THE WHOLE MATTER!

I DON'T CARE! SOMEBODY SHOULD BE HERE!

SOMEBODY WILL BE, DEAR. BILL IS SENDING OVER ONE OF HIS BEST YOUNG MEN TO KEEP AN EYE ON ME.

IS HE STOUT? RESOLUTE? WHERE DID HE GO TO SCHOOL?

GO! SCAT! YOU'LL MISS YOUR PLANE!

CERTAINLY IS GOOD TO SEE YOU GENTS BACK IN TEXAS! WHAT TIME WOULD YOU LIKE ME TO RUN YOU OVER TO THE ISLAND?

SOONER THE BETTER, BOB. I'M AFRAID WE'VE MISSED MOST OF THE BIRDS AS IT IS.

WELL, NOT ALL OF 'EM. I SEEN SOME PINTAILS TODAY. THERE'S EVEN SOME WHOOPERS. SINBAD IS STILL HERE, AND MATILDA..

HOW ABOUT IGGY? IS OL' IGGY STILL HERE?

UH..NOPE. I'M AFRAID I GOT SOME BAD NEWS THERE, RICHARD. IGGY HAD A ROUGH WINTER. HE'S..HE'S EXTINCT.

OH..NO! THAT'S TERRIBLE!

YOU MEAN, DEAD, DON'T YOU?

NO, IGGY WAS ONE OF A KIND, THADIUS.

HE WAS THE WHOOPING CRANE'S WHOOPING CRANE.

WE'RE IN LUCK, THAD. MATILDA'S STILL HERE, AND LOOK, THERE'S SAMPSON AND WALTER!

I DON'T KNOW HOW YOU KEEP THEM ALL STRAIGHT, DICK.

WELL, THERE ARE ONLY 73 WHOOPING CRANES ON MATAGORDA, THAD. BESIDES, THEY'RE AS INDIVIDUAL AS YOU AND I. COLOR, MARKINGS, BEHAVIOR PATTERNS, EACH BIRD HAS ITS OWN ECCENTRICITIES.

FOR INSTANCE, SAM THERE IS GAY. AND TILLY WON'T EAT WATER BEETLES UNLESS THEY'VE BEEN STRAINED, AND WALTER SPENDS A LOT OF TIME WITH THE DUCKS.

AND ALL THIS IS CONDONED BY THE WILDLIFE SERVICE?

IT'S A SANCTUARY, THAD.

I THINK I'M BEGINNING TO UNDERSTAND THE WHOOPING CRANE'S BRUSH WITH EXTINCTION.

BOY.. LOOK AT THOSE BEACHES! CAN YOU IMAGINE IF THIS ISLAND WERE RUN BY THE TEXAS PARKS COMMISSION?

BUT WASN'T THAT WATT'S ORIGINAL PLAN? WHY DO YOU SUPPOSE HE'S SETTLING FOR JOINT CONTROL?

HE HAD NO SUPPORT, THAD. WHEN THEY HELD HEARINGS HERE, 37 OF THE 38 WITNESSES WERE AGAINST THE TRANSFER!

THAT'S THE MAN'S MAIN PROBLEM, THAD. WHETHER IT'S LAND DEVELOPMENT, OIL LEASES OR TIMBER RIGHTS, WATT PUSHES SUCH EXTREME PLANS, EVEN THE INTENDED BENEFICIARIES ARE NONPLUSSED.

BY AN EMBARRASSMENT OF RICHES, AS IT WERE.

RIGHT. MOST COMPANIES JUST AREN'T GEARED UP FOR RAPE.

I JUST DON'T UNDERSTAND WATT, DICK. WHAT DO YOU SUPPOSE MAKES A MAN LIKE THAT TICK?

VERY SIMPLE, THAD, HE'S A ZEALOT. HE REALLY BELIEVES HE'S ON A MISSION FROM GOD.

IT'S MADE HIM VERY HIGH-STRUNG AND BRITTLE. EVER NOTICE HOW HE LAUGHS AT ALL THE WRONG TIMES, THE WAY NIXON USED TO? YOU HAVE THE SENSE HE COULD BREAK AT ANY MOMENT.

YEAH, BUT WHY IS HE TAKING IT ALL OUT AGAINST THE ENVIRONMENT?

WELL, I HEARD THAT WHEN HE WAS FOUR, HE WAS ATTACKED BY A FLOCK OF STARLINGS.

INCREDIBLE. IT'S ALMOST LIKE BIRDS HAVE A SPECIAL SENSE.

AFTER THAT, HE NEVER REALLY BELIEVED WHERE HE STOOD ON THE FOOD CHAIN.

I WONDER IF WE SHOULD BE TURNING BACK, DICK.

NO, LET'S GO A LITTLE FURTHER, THAD. I'D LIKE TO LOG A PELICAN TODAY IF I COULD.

IT'S NOT OFTEN WE GET TO BIRD IN SUCH PRISTINE SURROUNDINGS. IT'S HARD TO BELIEVE WE'RE SO CLOSE TO CIVILIZATION.

I KNOW. DO YOU REALIZE WE'VE WALKED FIVE HOURS WITHOUT SEEING A SOUL?

INCREDIBLE, ISN'T IT?

GREASE 'EM! GREASE 'EM!

SHUT UP, BIRD! THEY'RE NOT IN RANGE!

WHAT TRIBE DO YOU THINK THEY'RE FROM, SIR?

FREEZE RIGHT THERE, GRAMPS!

HO, THADIUS! RUN FOR IT! I'M TAKEN!

HOLD IT, FELLAH! GET BACK HERE, OR YOUR PAL'S A DEAD MAN!

HE OWES YOU A LOT OF MONEY, I ASSUME.

NO, NO, HE'S JUST HARD OF HEARING.

..AND YOU WEREN'T SENT HERE BY THE FEDS TO TRACK ME DOWN?

HEAVENS, NO. I'M JUST A TOURIST VISITING THE ISLAND.

TOURIST, HUH? THEN WHAT WERE YOU DOING SNEAKING AROUND THE DUNES?

BY AVOCATION, I'M A BIRD-WATCHER, SIR. BIRDING REQUIRES STEALTH.

I DON'T GET IT, GRAMPS. WHAT'S A BIRD-WATCHER DOING IN THE MIDDLE OF A..WAR ZONE?

WAR ZONE? MY DEAR BOY, THIS IS THE ISLAND OF MATAGORDA, OFF OF TEXAS!

TEXAS?

AMERICA, SIR! OUR ORDEAL IS OVER!

NOT NECESSARILY. THERE MAY NOT BE ENOUGH ROOM IN THE BOAT.

..AND WHILE I WAS TRYING TO QUELL THE MUTINY, WE HIT THIS DAMN REEF!

IT WASN'T HIS FAULT, THOUGH. THE CHART WAS NEARLY THREE YEARS OUT OF DATE.

AND WHO MIGHT YOU BE, YOUNG LADY?

I MIGHT BE HONEY, SIR. I WAS THE PURSER ON THE "RUSTY NAIL". NOW I'M MR. DUKE'S GAL FRIDAY.

REALLY? ARE YOU SURE YOU'D LIKE TO BE RESCUED, MR. DUKE? MOST MEN DREAM OF BEING SHIPWRECKED ON AN ISLAND WITH A CHARMING YOUNG LADY!

HELL, SO DO I, BUT HONEY AND I WERE THE ONLY SURVIVORS.

COMPLIMENT RECEIVED ON THIS END, SIR.

HARD TO BELIEVE, ISN'T IT, HONEY? DOWN TO OUR LAST WEEK'S RATION OF TEQUILA, AND WE'RE RESCUED BY A COUPLE OF BIRD-WATCHERS!

I WAS BEGINNING TO THINK WE WERE DONE FOR, WEREN'T YOU, HONEY?

NOT REALLY, SIR. I WAS PRETTY SURE WE'D MAKE IT.

OH, YEAH? HOW COME?

UM..WELL, ACTUALLY, I HAVE A SMALL CONFESSION, SIR. I SAW THE FERRY COME OVER HERE ABOUT A MONTH AGO.

SAY WHAT?

I JUST THOUGHT IT MORE IMPORTANT THAT WE HAVE SOME TIME TO OURSELVES.

HOW MUCH LONGER BEFORE THE FERRY GETS HERE, SIR?

IT SHOULD BE HERE MOMENTARILY. ANXIOUS TO BE LEAVING, ARE YOU?

ACTUALLY, SIR, I'M A LITTLE AMBIVALENT. DUKE AND I HAD SOME WONDERFUL TIMES HERE.

I GUESS I'M ALSO A LITTLE LET DOWN. WHEN WE FIRST ARRIVED, I CLAIMED THE ISLAND FOR CHINA. I THOUGHT I'D DISCOVERED A NEW VACATION SPOT FOR THE MASSES TO COME TO.

YOU CLAIMED MATAGORDA FOR CHINA?

WELL, MOST OF IT. I LOST THE MINERAL RIGHTS TO DUKE IN A POKER GAME.

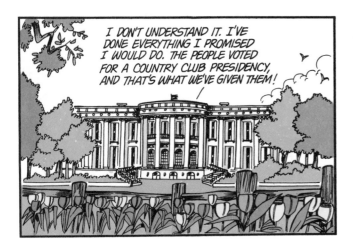

..AND AFTER I LOST MY CAMERA-MAN, THE BUREAU DECIDED I COULD USE A LITTLE TIME STATESIDE. SO I GRABBED THE NEXT CHOPPER OUT.

IT'S NOT A BAD LIFE. BUT IT CERTAINLY PRESENTS ONE WITH SOME INTERESTING LAUNDRY PROBLEMS.

I CAN IMAGINE.

FOR INSTANCE, TAKE THESE PESKY BLOODSTAINS ON MY BEST SAFARI SHIRT..

BLOODSTAINS? NOT ANOTHER FIREFIGHT IN BEIRUT?

NO, A SAVAGE BEATING IN ARGENTINA. FOR REPORTING THE TRUTH AS I SAW IT.

HMM..HAVE YOU TRIED LEMON JUICE?

FINISHED UP, HAVE WE?

WE SEEM TO HAVE.

WELL, IT'S BEEN GREAT SPINNING AND DRYING WITH YOU. WHAT DID YOU SAY YOUR NAME WAS?

JOANIE. JOANIE CAUCUS.

NICE TO MEET YOU, JOAN.

THANK YOU. IT'S CERTAINLY BEEN INTERESTING MEETING YOU.

I'D FOLLOW THROUGH, BUT I LEAVE ON A MISSION TONIGHT.

THAT'S OKAY. I HADN'T GOTTEN MY HOPES UP.

OKAY, CAMPERS, IT'S CURRENT EVENTS NIGHT AGAIN, SO LET'S PUT ON OUR THINKING CAPS! TONIGHT'S TOPIC, "REAGAN: A MAN AND HIS VACATIONS."

ON THE HOT SEAT TONIGHT, HERE TO DISCUSS FIRST FAMILY FROLICS, IS EVERETT WANAMAKER, WHITE HOUSE VACATION COORDINATOR! LET'S HOLD THOSE CALLS UNTIL OL' MARK'S HAD A SHOT AT THIS GUY, OKAY?

OKAY, EV, FIRST OF ALL, WHAT *IS* A VACATION COORDINATOR? WHAT DO YOU DO?

WELL, BASICALLY, MARK, I'M RESPONSIBLE FOR PACKAGING THE PRESIDENT'S VACATIONS SO THEY'RE PALATABLE TO THE PUBLIC.

UM..BEEN ON THE JOB LONG, HAVE YOU, EV?

NO, NO, I WAS BROUGHT IN AFTER THE BARBADOS DEBACLE.

SO LEVEL WITH US, EV, WHAT'S THE PRESIDENT'S VACATION STRATEGY THIS SUMMER?

VERY SIMPLE, MARK. MORE TRIPS, BUT OF SHORTER DURATION.

LAST SUMMER'S MONSTER VACATION WAS A BUST, SO WE'RE SPACING IT OUT. A WEEK HERE, A WEEK THERE. IT ADDS UP, OF COURSE, BUT NO ONE NOTICES.

OH, C'MON, YOU DON'T REALLY BELIEVE THE PUBLIC WILL FALL FOR THAT, DO YOU?

MARK, HOW MANY DAYS OF VACATION DO YOU THINK THE PRESIDENT HAS TAKEN SO FAR THIS YEAR?

UM.. I DUNNO. TEN?

NOPE. 114. BELIEVE ME, THE SYSTEM WORKS.

...AND, OF COURSE, HE'S GOT ANOTHER AUGUST VACATION COMING UP, WHICH THE PRESIDENT PROBABLY WON'T EVEN ENJOY BECAUSE HE'LL BE WORKING SO HARD.

OH? DOING WHAT?

MAKING TOUGH DECISIONS THAT ONLY HE, AS PRESIDENT, CAN MAKE.

I SEE. ANY OTHER BIG WORKING VACATIONS ON THE DRAWING BOARD?

WELL, IT'S SUPPOSED TO BE A SECRET, BUT HE'S THINKING OF TAKING NEXT YEAR OFF.

THE WHOLE YEAR?

THAT'S RIGHT. OF COURSE, HE'D BE IN CONSTANT TOUCH WITH THE WHITE HOUSE.

EV, LET'S TAKE THE GLOVES OFF, OKAY? GIVEN THE CURRENT HARD TIMES, DO YOU THINK REAGAN'S RELENTLESS VACATION SCHEDULE IS WINNING HIM ANY POINTS IN THE SENSITIVITY DEPARTMENT?

AS A MATTER OF FACT, MARK, I DO. YOU SEE, THE PRESIDENT GREW UP DURING THE DEPRESSION. HE REMEMBERS THE OLD HIGH SOCIETY MOVIES AND WHAT A GREAT ESCAPE THEY WERE FOR POOR PEOPLE..

THAT'S WHY HE TAKES OFF SO MUCH TIME. IT'S JUST MR. REAGAN'S WAY OF GETTING PEOPLE'S MINDS OFF THEIR PROBLEMS. THANKS TO TELEVISION, WHEN HE TAKES A VACATION, THE WHOLE COUNTRY GETS TO GO ALONG!

SOUNDS GREAT! WHERE ARE WE OFF TO NEXT?

BEVERLY HILLS! PALM SPRINGS! NEW YORK! YOU TELL US! THEY'RE YOUR VACATIONS, AMERICA!

EV, LET'S TALK FOR A MINUTE ABOUT ONE OF THE PRESIDENT'S MOST MEMORABLE VACATIONS— LAST SPRING'S DISASTROUS TRIP TO BARBADOS.

AS YOU KNOW, THOSE FEW DAYS OF R&R COST THE TAXPAYERS MILLIONS OF DOLLARS, AS WELL AS THE GOOD WILL OF SEVERAL CARIBBEAN LEADERS CYNICALLY ADDED TO THE SCHEDULE AS AN AFTERTHOUGHT..

MOREOVER, IT EXHAUSTED THE PRESIDENT, MAKING THE TRIP POINTLESS. ANY COMMENT?

HE ALSO RUINED HIS FILM AND GOT A SUNBURN. HEY, HAVEN'T YOU EVER HAD A VACATION WHERE EVERYTHING WENT WRONG?

PLAIN BAD LUCK, HUH?

LOOK, THE GUY'S HUMAN. HE EVEN LOST HIS TRAVELER'S CHECKS!

YEAH, LET ME SPEAK TO REAGAN'S VACATION MAN!

YOU GOT HIM, GUY!

LISTEN, MAN, WHAT I WANT TO KNOW IS WHY THE PRESIDENT'S TAKING ALL THESE VACATIONS WHEN 9% OF THE WORK FORCE IS ON PERMANENT VACATION, DIG? ANSWER ME THAT, MR. VACATION COORDINATOR!

I MEAN, I'VE BEEN OUT OF WORK SINCE APRIL, AND..

HEY, HEY, LIGHTEN UP, GUY! YOU MAY NOT BE WORKING RIGHT NOW, BUT LET ME ASK YOU THIS: HOW'S YOUR TAN? HUH?

I'M BLACK.

EXACTLY! SO THE SUMMER WASN'T A TOTAL LOSS, RIGHT?

HEY, MIKE, YOU SEEN BOOPSIE?

YEAH. SHE WENT DOWN TO THE OPENING OF THE NEW JANE FONDA FITNESS CENTER.

WHAT?

DIDN'T SHE TELL YOU? SHE SIGNED UP FOR SOME SESSIONS.

I DON'T BELIEVE THAT CHICK..

SHE WAS PRETTY EXCITED. JANE FONDA IS HERE TO LEAD THE FIRST WEEK OF WORKOUTS HERSELF!

BRAN! NUTS! GERM! SEED! WE DON'T WANT YOUR CORPORATE GREED!

>PUFF! PUFF!< AM I DOING IT RIGHT, MISS FONDA?

A LITTLE LOWER.. LOWER.. WHAT ARE YOU FEEL-ING?

I FEEL A BURN.. >PUFF!<.. BUT IT'S A GOOD BURN!

WHAT ELSE DO YOU FEEL?

I FEEL.. A SURGE OF PRIDE, OF SELF-ESTEEM.. I FEEL I'VE BEEN RIPPED OFF BY A FALSE FEMALE IDEAL!

WHAT ELSE? LISTEN TO YOUR BODY!

I FEEL.. SENSITIVE! NO, SENSITIZED! I FEEL POLITICALLY SENSITIZED!

GOOD! NOW THE OTHER SIDE!

WOW.. THAT WAS SOME WORKOUT, MISS FONDA..

WELL, I'M JUST TRYING TO KEEP WOMEN LIKE YOURSELVES FROM MAKING THE MISTAKES I DID..

IT TOOK ME 20 YEARS OF SELF-ABUSE, OF DIET GUM AND BINGEING AND VOMITING AND DEXEDRINE AND DIURET-ICS, BEFORE I LEARNED THE SECRET TO LOSING WEIGHT: EAT LESS AND EXERCISE MORE!

WOW..

GEE..

WHAT A BREAK-THROUGH.

HOW COME IT TOOK 20 YEARS?

MALE DOCTORS HID THE TRUTH FROM ME.

THERE YOU ARE! DO YOU KNOW WHAT TIME IT IS?

SORRY, B.D., BUT A GOOD WORKOUT TAKES TIME!

GOD, WILL YOU LOOK AT YOU! YOU'RE A MESS! SWEATING ALL OVER THE CARPET LIKE / SOME..

I MADE A BREAKTHROUGH TODAY, B.D...

ABOUT 40 MINUTES INTO THE WORK-OUT, I BEGAN TO FEEL REALLY GOOD ABOUT MYSELF! A FEW MINUTES LATER, IT SUDDENLY HIT ME THAT I'D SPENT MY WHOLE LIFE INTERNALIZING SOME DUMB FEMININE IDEAL!

GREAT.

MISS FONDA WAS AMAZED! I'M ONLY UP TO BEGINNER'S BUTTOCKS!

IT'S TRUE, B.D.! GETTING IN SHAPE AND POLITICAL ACTIVISM ARE RELATED!

WHAT GARBAGE! WERE THE SPARTANS POLITICALLY ACTIVE? ARE THE CINCINNATI BENGALS?

IF YOU LOOK AT YOUR HISTORY, ALL THE PEOPLE WHO PROMOTED PHYSICAL FITNESS THROUGH THE AGES HAVE BEEN CONSERVATIVE. BELIEVE ME, LIBERALS KNOW NOTHING ABOUT GETTING IN SHAPE, ESPECIALLY LADY LIBERALS!

OH, YEAH?

YEAH!

WHAT ABOUT THE BIKINI SCENE IN "GOLDEN POND"?

THAT WAS ALL SPECIAL EFFECTS! JEEZ, BOOPSIE, SOMETIMES YOU CAN BE SO GULLIBLE!

MISS FONDA, MY BOYFRIEND HAS BEEN GIVING ME A LOT OF GRIEF ABOUT YOUR PROGRAM. HE SAYS IT'S ONLY FOR THE TRENDY MIDDLE CLASS.

WELL, THAT MAY HAVE BEEN A PROBLEM IN THE PAST..

BUT STARTING THIS FALL, MY BEVERLY HILLS WORKOUT SALON WILL BE SETTING UP FITNESS OUT-REACH CLINICS TO HELP MIGRANT FARM WORKERS MEET THEIR EXERCISE NEEDS!

MIGRANT FARM WORKERS?

RIGHT.

DON'T THEY ALREADY GET ENOUGH EXERCISE?

ONLY IN THEIR UPPER ARMS. THEY COMPLETELY NEGLECT THOSE IMPORTANT ABDOMINALS.

HEY.. IS THAT A KNITTED BROW I SEE?

WHAT?

YOU'RE WORRYING ABOUT SOMETHING. WHICH IS FUNNY, BECAUSE I AM, TOO. WHAT ARE YOU WORRYING ABOUT?

OH.. NOTHING.

OH, YES, YOU ARE. I'LL BET IT'S THE SAME THING I'M WORRYING ABOUT. C'MON, TELL ME.

AMNIOCENTESIS.

OH.. NO, THAT'S NOT IT. I WAS WORRYING ABOUT THE CLUTCH ON THE VOLVO.

AMNIOCENTESIS? YOU'RE WORRIED ABOUT AMNIOCENTESIS?

OF COURSE, I'M WORRIED ABOUT IT. TOMORROW I HAVE TO GO IN FOR AN ABSOLUTELY DREADFUL PROCEDURE, FOLLOWING WHICH I STAND A 1-IN-50 CHANCE OF RECEIVING TERRIBLE NEWS.

MEANWHILE, I'M TURNING INTO THIS MISSHAPEN BLIMPO WITH PERSISTENT NAUSEA, PREMATURE BACKACHE, VIOLENT MOOD SWINGS..

HMM.. SOUNDS LIKE YOU COULD USE SOME CHEERING UP!

..AND A HUSBAND WHO KEEPS TRYING TO CHEER ME UP!

HEY, GIVE ME A CHANCE. I'VE GOT SOME NEW HAND SHADOWS.

..AND WE FEEL WE'VE BEEN MORE THAN FLEXIBLE DURING THE NEGOTIATIONS. THE DROPPING OF OUR DEMAND FOR A LIST OF P.L.O. EVACUEES IS A GOOD EXAMPLE.

BUT WHY DID YOU NEED SUCH A LIST IN THE FIRST PLACE?

TO MONITOR COMPLIANCE, OF COURSE. TO MAKE SURE ALL THE TERRORISTS LEFT.

BUT ONCE YOU HAD ALL THEIR NAMES AND ADDRESSES IN YOUR COMPUTER, COULDN'T THAT HAVE LED TO ALL KINDS OF ABUSE?

ABUSE? LIKE WHAT?

WELL, LIKE, WHAT WOULD'VE KEPT YOU FROM SENDING THE GUERRILLAS A LOT OF JUNK MAIL?

WE WERE PREPARED TO OFFER CERTAIN GUARANTEES.

I'M JUST DELIGHTED YOUR YOUNG MAN DOESN'T MIND MY BORROWING YOU FOR A FEW WEEKS, DEAR. IT'S SO DREARY CAMPAIGNING BY ONESELF.

I'M PLEASED, TOO, LACEY. IT'S NICE TO GET OUT OF WASHINGTON FOR A WHILE.

I'LL WANT YOU TO STAY AT OUR HOUSE, OF COURSE, AND YOU CAN USE THE LIBRARY AS YOUR OFFICE.

BASICALLY, YOUR RESPONSIBILITIES WILL BE TO SCHEDULE A FEW APPEARANCES AND ARRANGE A SMALL MEDIA CAMPAIGN. THAT'S ABOUT ALL YOU'D REALLY HAVE TO DO.

WHAT ABOUT RECRUITING CANVASSERS?

HMM.. TOO LATE FOR THAT. WE MIGHT HAVE TO USE THE SERVANTS AGAIN.

HI. IT'S THE PREGNANT LADY.

HI, PREGNANT LADY. HOW'S IT GOING OUT THERE?

PRETTY GOOD. I'M ALL SETTLED INTO MY NEW OFFICE, AND LACEY IS ALREADY OUT CAMPAIGNING.

I MUST SAY, IT'S REALLY AN EXPERIENCE WATCHING HER MEET WITH PEOPLE. SHE'S CERTAINLY NOT SHY ABOUT STANDING ON HER RECORD!

..AND HERE ARE SOME OF THE VOTES I'M PROUDEST OF.

HMM.. NOT BAD.

BOY! LOOKS LIKE YOU VOTED YOUR CONSCIENCE RIGHT DOWN THE LINE!

ANOTHER INVITE JUST CAME IN, BOSS. THE BAY AREA GAY ALLIANCE WOULD LIKE YOU TO SPEAK TO THEM TOMORROW.

THE GAY ALLIANCE?

ACTUALLY, YOU MIGHT WANT TO DO THAT ONE. I'VE BEEN LOOKING OVER THE LATEST DEMOGRAPHICS, AND YOUR DISTRICT IS NOW HEAVILY GAY.

GOODNESS! IT IS?

MY, HOW THINGS CHANGE! YES, BY ALL MEANS LET'S GO. I'D LOVE TO HEAR WHAT THEY HAVE TO SAY!

THAT'S RIGHT.

THAT'S VERY OPEN OF YOU, BOSS.

NOT AT ALL. I'VE ALWAYS FOUND CONFIRMED BACHELORS JUST SO FASCINATING!

MY! WHAT A NICE-LOOKING GROUP OF YOUNG PEOPLE!

YES, THEY.. ANDY!

HI, KID.

ANDY! I DON'T BELIEVE IT! WHAT ARE YOU DOING HERE?

I'M ONE OF THE ORGANIZERS OF THE BAY AREA GAY ALLIANCE.

LACEY, THIS IS ANDY, AN OLD FRIEND OF MINE. WE ONCE DATED. AT LEAST I THOUGHT WE WERE DATING.

IN OUR WAY, WE WERE.

I'M A LITTLE CONFUSED, DEAR.

SO WAS I.

WE HAD A LITTLE COMMUNICATION PROBLEM.

BOY, IT SURE IS GREAT TO SEE YOU AGAIN, JOANIE.

THIS IS A WONDERFUL SURPRISE FOR ME, TOO, ANDY.

YOU'RE WORKING ON THE DAVENPORT CAMPAIGN, I TAKE IT?

YUP. I'M HER CAMPAIGN MANAGER.

REALLY? THAT'S GREAT! GOOD LUCK TO BOTH OF YOU.

THANKS. WE'LL NEED IT.

SO. STILL HANGING OUT WITH STRAIGHTS, I SEE.

AFRAID SO. IT'S MY HUSBAND'S INFLUENCE.

SO HOW LONG HAVE YOU BEEN WORKING FOR CONGRESSWOMAN DAVENPORT?

EVER SINCE WE MOVED TO WASHINGTON.

SHE CERTAINLY SEEMS LIKE A REMARKABLE WOMAN.

OH, SHE IS, ANDY, SHE REALLY IS..

I'M NOT SURE HOW MUCH SHE KNOWS ABOUT HER NEW GAY CONSTITUENCY, BUT SHE'S CERTAINLY WILLING TO LEARN.

BUT HAVE YOU TRIED, I MEAN, REALLY TRIED, DATING GIRLS YOUR OWN AGE?

IT DOESN'T QUITE WORK THAT WAY, MA'AM.

I MUST SAY, DEARS, THIS LITTLE CHAT HAS BEEN MOST ENLIGHTENING. I HAD NO IDEA THE GAY COMMUNITY WAS FACING SO MANY PROBLEMS.

AS YOU CAN IMAGINE, THIS IS ALL NEW GROUND FOR ME. WE NEVER HAD ANY GAYS AMONG OUR FAMILY AND FRIENDS.

WELL, NOW, ACTUALLY, THAT'S NOT TRUE. DICK'S UNCLE ORVILLE CAME OUT OF THE CLOSET LAST YEAR. HE'S A FEDERAL JUDGE IN CHICAGO.

THAT'S GREAT! WHAT MADE HIM DO IT?

HIGH INTEREST RATES. HIS BUTLER TRIED TO BLACKMAIL HIM, AND HE COULDN'T AFFORD IT.

I'D LIKE TO THANK THE GAY ALLIANCE FOR INVITING ME HERE TONIGHT. CHATTING WITH ALL OF YOU HAS BEEN MOST INSTRUCTIVE.

ALSO, I MUST SAY, IT'S REFRESHING TO MEET A GROUP OF CONSTITUENTS WITH SUCH FINE MANNERS. I'M ALSO VERY IMPRESSED WITH HOW NICELY YOU ALL DRESS.

THE ONLY THING I MIGHT QUIBBLE WITH IS YOUR HAIR. SOME OF YOU BOYS HAVE TERRIBLY SHORT HAIRCUTS. HAIR THAT SHORT LOOKS FINE ON NAVY CADETS, BUT OTHERWISE IT MAKES YOU LOOK AWFULLY YOUNG.

UH.. LACEY..

NEVER MIND. MINOR POINT. THANKS AGAIN.

IT'S NO USE. ACCORDING TO MY CALCULATIONS, THERE'S JUST NO WAY OUT OF IT THIS TIME!

OUT OF WHAT, ZONK?

GRADUATION. THE ONLY THING BETWEEN ME AND THE REAL WORLD IS ONE UNFLUNKABLE CERAMICS COURSE!

GOOD. THEN YOU CAN COME IN WITH ME TODAY AND SIGN UP FOR SOME JOB INTER-VIEWS.

JOB INTERVIEWS?

UH-HUH.

LET ME RECHECK MY FIGURES.

MAYBE YOU CAN BREAK THE KILN.

JOB INTERVIEWS? YOU'RE ACTUALLY SIGNING UP FOR JOB INTERVIEWS?

WE'RE SENIORS, ZONK. WHAT OTHER CHOICE DO WE HAVE?

BUT I DON'T KNOW THE FIRST THING ABOUT JOB INTERVIEWS! I'D BE EATEN ALIVE!

NO, YOU WOULDN'T, ZONK..

IT'S REALLY NO BIG DEAL.. YOU JUST TALK TO THE RECRUITER FOR TWENTY MINUTES OR SO. ALL YOU HAVE TO DO IS BE YOUR-SELF.

BUT.. BUT WHAT IF THEY OFFER ME A JOB?

WELL, YOU ALWAYS RUN THAT RISK.

NAME?

HARRIS, ZONKER.

WHICH COMPANIES ARE YOU INTERESTED IN INTERVIEWING WITH?

DEPENDS. WHAT HAVE YOU GOT?

MR. HARRIS, THERE ARE OVER 200 COMPANIES RE-CRUITING ON CAMPUS. WHAT ARE YOUR GEN-ERAL AREAS OF INTEREST?

AERODYNAMICS. DESIGNER JEANS. ROOFING SUPPLIES. THAT SORT OF THING.

WHAT SORT OF THING?

YOU KNOW, LIQUIDITY. POINT-OF-SALE. MARGIN AC-COUNTS. FAST LANE.

CAREFUL, ZONK. YOU'LL PEAK BEFORE THE INTERVIEWS.

MR. HARRIS, I'VE BEEN LOOKING OVER YOUR ACADEMIC TRANSCRIPT, AND I'VE BEEN TRYING TO FIND THE RIGHT WORD TO DESCRIBE YOUR CAREER HERE..

"CHECKERED" COMES TO MIND, OF COURSE. "DISASTROUS" ALSO SUGGESTS ITSELF, AS DOES "CATASTROPHIC"..

HOW ABOUT "COLORFUL"? OR PERHAPS "REMARKABLE"?

YES, THOSE ARE APPLICABLE. "COLORFUL" CERTAINLY REFLECTS THE SPIRIT OF YOUR RECORD. AND WHO COULD ARGUE WITH "REMARKABLE"?

WHO INDEED?

AND YET, "CATASTROPHIC" STAYS WITH ME..

YOU'RE FIXATING. PUT IT ASIDE FOR A WHILE.

SO HOW LONG HAVE YOU BEEN INTERESTED IN SOFTWARE, MR. HARRIS?

MY WHOLE LIFE. FROM JEANS TO T-SHIRTS TO EARTH SHOES, I'VE ALWAYS BEEN PARTIAL TO COMFORTABLE CLOTHES.

HEE, HEE, THAT'S GREAT! YOU DON'T TAKE THE BUSINESS WORLD VERY SERIOUSLY, DO YOU, MR. HARRIS?

UM.. WELL..

I LIKE THAT KIND OF IRREVERENCE, MR. HARRIS. FRANKLY, IT'S DAMN REFRESHING!

IT IS?

WHEN CAN YOU START?

UM.. YOU'LL HAVE TO TALK TO MY AGENT.

HEY! HE'S BACK! HOW DID IT GO?

DON'T ASK.

LISTEN, MIKE, I HAVE AN IDEA. LET'S BREAK INTO THE REGISTRAR'S OFFICE AND TAMPER WITH OUR RECORDS AND MAKE OURSELVES JUNIORS AGAIN.

THAT BAD, HUH?

WORSE. ONE GUY ACTUALLY TRIED TO GIVE ME A JOB. IF I HADN'T PUT DOWN A FAKE NAME, I'D BE EMPLOYED RIGHT NOW!

YOU BETTER SIT DOWN. YOU LOOK A LITTLE SHOOK UP.

YOU TOLD ME THERE WEREN'T ANY JOBS, MIKE. YOU LIED TO ME!

MARILOU! GREAT NEWS!

GOODNESS, WHAT IS IT, DEAR?

THE BOARD JUST VOTED ME THE NEW CHAIRMAN!

CHAIRMAN? OF THE ENTIRE COMPANY?

THE WHOLE STORE! NOW I CAN ORDER TAKEOVERS! SELL OFF DIVISIONS! HAVE EXECUTIVES TAKEN OUT AND SHOT! I'M ONE OF THE **BIG BOYS** NOW!

I'VE ALWAYS THOUGHT OF YOU AS A BIG BOY, DEAR.

I'VE GOT TO CALL MY MENTOR. WHAT'S THE NUMBER OVER AT THE NURSING HOME?

HOW'S THE TAKEOVER GOING, WALT?
LOOKS PROMISING. WE THINK WE'VE GOT A CLEAR LINE ON 55% OF TRENDEX'S STOCK..

I'M TRYING TO FIND A BUYER FOR THEIR PAINT DIVISION. IF WE GET CONTROL, PHIL WANTS TO DUMP IT FAST TO IMPROVE OUR CASH POSITION. HE'S ALSO GOING TO FIRE ALL OF TRENDEX'S EXECS.

BOY.. DOES THEIR PRESIDENT KNOW WHAT WE'RE UP TO YET?
HE WILL IN A MINUTE. PHIL'S IN THE OTHER ROOM CALLING HIM NOW.

..AND PEG AND THE KIDS ARE FINE? GREAT! LISTEN, FRED, I'LL TELL YOU WHY I CALLED..

MOM, WHAT'S ALL THIS I'VE BEEN HEARING ON THE NEWS ABOUT DAD MAKING A GRAB FOR TRENDEX?
YOUR FATHER'S DOING WHAT HE THINKS IS IN THE BEST INTERESTS OF THE FIRM, DEAR.

I'LL BET. IT LOOKS LIKE ANOTHER INSANE POWER PLAY TO ME. WHERE IS DAD? I HAVEN'T BEEN ABLE TO REACH HIM AT THE OFFICE.
HE'S HOLED UP IN A MOTEL IN STAMFORD UNTIL THE DEAL GOES THROUGH, DEAR.

I TRIED TO TAKE HIM SOME SOUP, BUT YOUR FATHER THINKS THE CORPORATE BATTLEGROUND IS NO PLACE FOR SPOUSES. THE ONLY WOMEN ALLOWED IN ARE BEAUTIFUL YOUNG PROTEGES.

HMM.. MAYBE I BETTER GO TALK TO HIM MYSELF.
NOW, DEAR, THOSE PROTEGES WILL BE VERY BUSY.

LOOKS LIKE TRENDEX HAS BROUGHT IN A WHITE KNIGHT, BOSS! JUST GOT WORD THAT SPANCO'S GOING FOR OUR STOCK!
DAMN! I WAS AFRAID FRED MIGHT TRY THAT! WE BETTER LOOK FOR SOMEONE TO BLOCK THEM!

I DON'T GET IT, DAD. WHY ARE YOU DOING THIS?!
TO PROVE THAT CAPITALISM STILL WORKS, MARK, TO SHOW THAT FREE MARKET FORCES STILL FAVOR THE CASH-RICH!

IT'S TIME THAT CAPTAINS OF INDUSTRY STOPPED ACTING LIKE TOTAL WIMPS! IF WE'RE TO KEEP AMERICAN BUSINESS STRONG, COMPANIES LIKE TRENDEX AND PEOPLE LIKE FRED BATES HAVE TO BE SACRIFICED!

BUT WHAT DID UNCLE FRED EVER DO TO YOU?
UNCLE FRED?
THIS IS NO TIME FOR SENTIMENTALITY! THE ECONOMY'S AT STAKE HERE!

EVERY NOW AND THEN, WE ON "LATE NIGHT" LIKE TO INVITE A BUSINESS TYCOON ON THE SHOW, AND SO WE DO. RIGHT, PAUL?
YOU'RE A FRESH KICK, DAVE! YOU KILL ME!

THANKS, PAUL. WITH US HERE TONIGHT IS MOGUL-IN-THE-NEWS PHIL SLACKMEYER. PHIL, WHAT'S THE STORY ON THIS BIG MERGER WITH TRENDEX?
IT'S NOT A MERGER, MR. LETTERMAN. IT'S CORPORATE WAR.

AHA. SO WE'RE TALKING ABOUT AN UNFRIENDLY TAKEOVER HERE, I'M GUESSING. NOW, WHAT'LL YOU DO TO TRENDEX IF YOU GET IT?
ROUGHLY WHAT ROME DID TO CARTHAGE. WE'LL ABSORB THEIR OPERATIONS AND RAZE THEIR CORPORATE STRUCTURE! TRENDEX WILL CEASE TO EXIST!

AMAZING. SAY, COULD WE GET A TIGHT SHOT OF THE VEINS ON PHIL'S NECK HERE?
WOMEN AND CHILDREN WILL BE PROVIDED FOR, OF COURSE..

GOOD NEWS, SIR. I THINK I'VE FOUND OUR OWN WHITE KNIGHT: UNIVERSAL PETROLEUM!

GOOD WORK, ADAMS. I LIKE YOUR INITIATIVE. HOW'D YOU LIKE TO BECOME MY NEW PRESIDENT, EFFECTIVE NOW?

WOULD I? BOY! I MOST CERTAINLY WOULD, SIR! I WON'T LET YOU DOWN!

FINE. I'M GOING TO NEED A GOOD HATCHET MAN IN THE DAYS AHEAD. WITH THE STAKES THIS HIGH, WE'RE EITHER GOING TO COME OUT OF THIS HEROES OR GO DOWN IN FLAMES!

OH..

ACTUALLY, SIR, I WONDER IF I COULD HAVE MY OLD JOB BACK.

DAMMIT, ADAMS, I WON'T TOLERATE FAILURE OF NERVE! YOU'RE FIRED!

ANY WAY YOU LOOK AT IT, JIM, IT'S A GOLDEN OPPORTUNITY. IF YOU AND UNIVERSAL PETROLEUM COME ON BOARD WITH US, WE CAN SNAP UP BOTH TRENDEX AND SPANCO!

WITH YOUR CLOUT AT THE BANKS, THERE'S NO WAY THEY COULD STOP US! THEIR STOCK IS SO UNDERVALUED NOW, IT'S A JOKE!

ACTUALLY, PHIL, FROM THE LOOKS OF THESE FIGURES, I'D SAY ALL THREE OF YOUR COMPANIES ARE RIPE FOR ACQUISITION.

JIM.. YOU WOULDN'T!

I CERTAINLY APPRECIATE YOUR BRINGING THIS TO MY ATTENTION, PHIL.

I DON'T UNDERSTAND, DEAR. WHATEVER HAPPENED?

I LOST THE COMPANY, THAT'S WHAT HAPPENED! ANDREWS DOUBLE-CROSSED ME AND GRABBED ALL THREE FIRMS!

WHAT THE HELL EVER HAPPENED TO ETHICS IN BUSINESS?

LOOK AT THE BRIGHT SIDE, DAD. YOU DESCENDED INTO THE VALLEY OF THE GREEDHEADS AND RETURNED IN ONE PIECE!

WHAT WILL YOU DO NOW, DEAR?

REAL ESTATE. I'M SWITCHING TO REAL ESTATE.

MONDO CONDO!

YOU WON'T DO THIS TO YOUR FAMILY AGAIN, WILL YOU, DEAR?

RAY! GOOD TO HEAR FROM YOU! HOW'S EVERYTHING OVER AT LABOR?

JUST FINE, MR. PRESIDENT. I WAS CALLING TO SEE IF YOU COULD COME TO MY "SALUTE TO RAY DONOVAN" DINNER.

"GUESS WHO'S GOING TO DINNER"

1982 SCENE   10 TAKE

GOSH, RAY, I THOUGHT YOU'D ALREADY HAD THAT DINNER..

YES, SIR, BUT IT WAS SUCH A HIT I DECIDED TO HAVE ANOTHER ONE TOMORROW NIGHT.

TOMORROW NIGHT? DARN THE LUCK, I'M AFRAID I'M BUSY TOMORROW. IF ONLY IT WERE WEDNESDAY..

NO SWEAT, SIR. I'M HAVING ANOTHER ONE WEDNESDAY. IT'S SORT OF A SERIES.

A SERIES OF SALUTES?

YES, SIR. A LOT OF PEOPLE HAVEN'T BEEN ABLE TO MAKE THE FIRST TWO.

FRIENDS, AS YOU KNOW, THE LAST 20 MONTHS HAVE BEEN A TERRIBLE ORDEAL FOR ME. BUT I THINK IT'S NOW TIME TO LET BYGONES BE BYGONES. EVEN THOUGH IT MEANS PUTTING DOZENS OF PERJURERS BACK ON THE STREETS.

IN THAT SPIRIT, I'VE ALSO DECIDED TO CALL OFF MY FORMER COMPANY'S IN-VESTIGATION OF THE SENATORS INVESTI-GATING ME. I'M GIVING ORRIN HATCH AND THE REST OF THE COMMITTEE A CLEAN BILL OF HEALTH!

NOW THAT'S CLASS!

WHAT A GUY!

ALSO, TO THANK ALL THE ELECTED OFFI-CIALS HERE TONIGHT, I PROMISE TO EN-DORSE EACH OF YOU FOR RE-ELECTION!

NO! NO! THAT'S OKAY!

WOULDN'T HEAR OF IT RAY!

THANKS ANY-WAY!

SIGH..

HI, SAILOR! WELCOME TO THE NEIGHBORHOOD. THE NAME'S ALICE P. SCHWARTZMAN! WHO ARE YOU?

UH..DUKE, THE NAME'S DUKE.

PLEASED TO MEET YOU, DUCK. WANT PART OF MY PAPER? IT'S ONLY THREE WEEKS OLD!

YEAH.. YOU GOT THE SPORTS SECTION?

SURE. YOU FOLLOW THE PONIES?

NAH. I JUST PUT MY LAST TEN BUCKS ON THE BREWERS.

THIS AIN'T YOUR DAY, DUCKS.

HEY, WHO'S THIS JOHN DE LOREAN GUY WHO'S ALL OVER THE PAPERS?

HE'S A BIG CAR EXECU-TIVE WHO GOT BUSTED FOR TRYING TO BUY A TON OF COCAINE.

OH..

HOW A SMART, GOOD-LOOKING FELLAH LIKE THAT COULD GET IN SO MUCH TROUBLE IS BEYOND ME!

WHAT A LIFE HE HAD, DUCKS! A GOLDEN BOY AT G.M., THREE GORGEOUS WIVES, THEN HIS OWN CAR COMPANY! SOMEBODY OUGHT TO MAKE A MOVIE OF HIS STORY. IT'D MAKE MILLIONS!

HELLO?

OF COURSE, THAT PERSON WOULD HAVE TO KNOW SOMETHING ABOUT THE DRUG WORLD.

A MOVIE! THAT'S A HELLUVA IDEA, LADY! "THE JOHN DE LOREAN STORY" IS A NATURAL!

TOO BAD YOU DON'T HAVE THE RIGHTS, DUCKY.

I CAN GET 'EM! I'LL CALL HIS LAWYER. I KNOW THIS WORLD — FAST CARS, CHEAP DRUGS, CHEAP CARS, AND FAST WOMEN — THIS IS MY SCENE!

GOOD LORD, I EVEN KNOW SOME OF THE PRINCIPALS! HETRICK AND ARRINGTON, THE TWO GUYS BUSTED WITH DE LOREAN! WE USED TO DOCK AT THE SAME WHARF IN FT. LAUDERDALE!

HELL, I EVEN ONCE LOANED THEM MY DECK GUN!

OKAY, I'M IN! HERE'S A DIME FOR THE CALL!

DUCKS! HOW'S OUR PROJECT COMING!

IT'S ON FIRE, ALICE. IT'S REALLY TAKING / OFF!

SID'S SO HIGH ON THE PROJECT HE GOT THE AGENCY TO GIVE ME AN OFFICE, THEY'RE EVEN ADVANCING ME PRE-PRODUCTION MONEY!

WE'LL BE MAKING A STUDIO DEAL THIS WEEK, I'LL DO THE SCRIPT NEXT WEEK, AND WE'LL START SHOOTING IN JANUARY. BY NEXT CHRISTMAS, WE'LL BOTH BE MILLION-AIRES!

GREAT! ACQUIRED THE RIGHTS YET?

NO, I'VE BEEN TOO BUSY. THERE'S BEEN A TON OF DETAILS!

SO WHEN DO WE MEET WITH THE STUDIO HEADS, SID?

WE START TOMOR-ROW, KID! WE'RE TAKING A LUNCH AT "MA MAISON" WITH MARTY FELBERG!

WHO'S MARTY FELBERG?

AN OLD FRIEND OF MINE. HE'S ABSOLUTELY HOT FOR YOUR PROJECT!

WHAT'S THE POOP ON HIM?

HE'S BIG, VERY BIG. HE CAN MAKE THINGS HAPPEN. BUT IF YOU CROSS HIM, HE'LL CRUSH YOU AND SEND YOU BACK TO KANSAS, WHETHER YOU CAME FROM THERE OR NOT!

HOW ABOUT IF HE LIKES YOU?

SKY'S THE LIMIT! COCAINE, SEX, LOANS AT 1/2% BELOW PRIME..

SID, I GOTTA TELL YOU, YOUR BOY IS PUTTING ME AWAY! I'M SITTING HERE LISTENING AND I'M NOT BELIEVING MY EARS!

HOLD ON TO YOUR HAT, MARTY. HE'S SAVED THE BEST FOR LAST!

GO AHEAD, DUKE, LAY IT ON HIM! TELL MARTY YOUR CAST-ING IDEA!

I'D LIKE TO GET DE LOREAN'S WIFE, CRISTINA FERRARE, TO PLAY HERSELF IN THE MOVIE.

MRS. DE LOREAN.. TO PLAY.. HERSELF? ARE YOU FOR REAL?

IS THAT BOLD, MARTY? WOULD THAT BE A COUP? IS THIS MAN A COMPLETE MANIAC?

He's out-rageous! Get outta here, you maniac!

DIDN'T I TELL YOU HE GAVE GREAT MEETING?

UH-HUH. I STILL DON'T SEE ANY MONEY ON THE TABLE.

OKAY, MARTY, I HATE TO PUT THE ARM ON YOU, BABE, BUT I GOTTA KNOW IF THIS IS A GO PROJECT FOR YOU PEOPLE!

HEY, SID, LIGHTEN UP! I TOLD YOU WE'D BE SWEETHEARTS, DIDN'T I?

THEN WE'RE TALKING GREEN LIGHT? YOU RAN IT UP THE FLAG-POLE AND THE MONEY SALUTED?

THE MONEY LOVED IT! YOUR SCRIPT IS THE TURN-ON OF THE YEAR!

MY SCRIPT?

IT'S SOLID GOLD, KID. EVERYONE AT THE STUDIO ATE IT UP! YOU'VE GOT ONE HELL OF A PAGE-TURNER ON YOUR HANDS!

BUT I HAVEN'T WRITTEN IT YET.

HEY, NO SWEAT. THIS THING WILL WRITE ITSELF!

YOU ROCCO?

MAYBE. WHO WANTS TO KNOW?

DUKE. LEO SENT ME. I UNDERSTAND YOU HAVE SOME MERCHANDISE TO SHOW ME.

YOU GOT THE MONEY?

WOULD I COME ALL THE WAY OUT HERE IF I DIDN'T?

OKAY, ROOM 101, CORAL MOTEL, ACROSS THE STREET. IN TEN MINUTES.

EXCUSE ME, WHAT'S HE SELLING? CAN I GET SOME, TOO?

ABORT.

SORRY. ONE-TIME OFFER.

MY, OH MY! ALL THAT NOSE CANDY FOR ME?

THAT'S RIGHT, MAN. 10 KILOS TO YOU FROM BOGOTA WITH LOVE!

10 KILOS? HOLD IT, PAL, IT WAS SUPPOSED TO BE 12 KILOS!

INFLATION, MAN! A HALF MIL JUST DON'T BUY WHAT IT USED TO..

INFLATION? WHAT SORT OF GARBAGE IS THAT?

IT'S A VERY POPULAR ITEM, MAN. EVERY TIME THERE'S A COKE JOKE ON THE "TONIGHT SHOW," DEMAND JUMPS 10%.

BUT CARSON'S BEEN ON VACATION ALL MONTH!

YEAH, BUT HIS GUEST HOSTS HAVE ALL BEEN DOING DE LOREAN.

WELL, EVERYTHING SEEMS TO BE IN ORDER HERE..

WE AIM TO PLEASE, MAN.

HEY, WAIT A MINUTE, PAL! THIS ISN'T ANYWHERE NEAR A HALF MIL!

RIGHT. IT'S FIFTY GRAND, A DOWN PAYMENT. YOU'LL GET THE REST AFTER I MOVE THE STUFF.

WHAT? I DON'T BELIEVE THIS! YOU ARE REALLY DUMB, YOU KNOW THAT, MAN? YOU ARE UNBELIEVABLY DUMB!

TAKE IT OR LEAVE IT, FELLAH.

IF THIS WERE A REAL COKE DEAL, YOU'D BE A DEAD MAN!

A REAL COKE DEAL?

SSHH! NOT YET!

IT'S BEEN GREAT DOING BUSINESS WITH YOU, FELLAHS. I'LL SEND YOU TICKETS TO THE PREMIERE!

I WOULDN'T GO COUNTING YOUR OSCARS QUITE YET, MR. DUKE.

WHAT DO YOU MEAN BY THAT, PAL?

LET'S PUT IT THIS WAY. WHAT'S THE WORST POSSIBLE NEWS YOU COULD RECEIVE RIGHT NOW?

YOU BURNED ME! YOU CREEPS SOLD ME 10 KILOS OF SUGAR!

NOPE. WORSE THAN THAT.

GOOD GUESS, THOUGH. TRY AGAIN.

YOU'RE COPS.

CLOSE ENOUGH?

ACTUALLY, FBI. BUT WE'LL GIVE IT TO YOU.

OKAY, WHAT WE'RE GOING TO DO NOW IS LISTEN TO A TAPE OF A NORMAL CHILDBIRTH. THE SOUNDS SHOULD HELP YOU PICTURE YOURSELVES IN THE DELIVERY ROOM.

AANH! AANH! PUFF!

THE MOTHER HAS GONE INTO HER FINAL CON-TRACTIONS AND IS BEARING DOWN!

DEEP BREATH! BEAR DOWN! HERE IT COMES!

THAT'S THE MONITRICE COACHING THE MOTHER.

MY GOD! HIS HEAD LOOKS LIKE A MELON!

THAT'S THE FATHER.

I JUST DON'T SEE WHY YOU CAN'T TAKE IT A LITTLE MORE SERIOUSLY, LIKE THE OTHER HUSBANDS..

I'M TRYING, JOANIE, I'M REALLY TRYING..

IT'S JUST I'VE NEVER DONE ANYTHING LIKE LAMAZE BEFORE. IT'S A LITTLE MORE THAN I BARGAINED FOR.

WHAT DO YOU MEAN? LIKE WHAT?

WELL, LIKE THAT MOVIE OF AN AC-TUAL BIRTH THEY SHOWED US. IT WAS SO.. WELL, GRAPHIC.

RICK, IT'S SUPPOSED TO BE GRAPHIC!

I DUNNO.. THE BROCHURE ONLY EMPHASIZED THE WOMAN'S SMIL-ING FACE.

HI, REV! WHAT'S COOKIN'?

I JUST DROPPED BY TO TELL YOU, MIKE — MY PEACE NEWSLETTER FINALLY GOT APPROVED!

NO KIDDING? THE DIOCESE WENT FOR IT?

YUP! I THINK THE BISHOPS' NUCLEAR FREEZE DEBATE HAD SOMETHING TO DO WITH IT.

I'VE ALREADY GOT VOLUNTEERS TO HELP EDIT, AND I'VE FOUND AN OFFICE AND A PRINTER. I STILL LACK ONE THING, THOUGH, AND IT'S GOT ME WORRIED.

DIVINE GUIDANCE?

NO, A WORD PROCESSOR. WILL YOU GO WITH ME TO THE STORE?

I DON'T KNOW WHY YOU WANT ME TO HELP YOU BUY A WORD PROCESSOR, REV. I KNOW LESS ABOUT THEM THAN YOU!

I'VE GOT COMPUTER PHOBIA, MIKE. COM-PUTERS ARE A WHOLE NEW, FRIGHTENING WORLD!

THEY'RE ALSO EX-PENSIVE, REV. DOES YOUR NU-CLEAR FREEZE NEWSLETTER HAVE THAT LARGE A BUDGET?

NOPE, I'LL PROBABLY HAVE TO SELL SUB-SCRIPTIONS TO COVER THE PAY-MENTS.

OR HAWK COPIES AT DEMON-STRATIONS.

I DON'T MIND. I'M LIKE THE FRANCISCANS. I DEPEND HEAVILY UPON THE KINDNESS OF STRANGERS.

SOME PEOPLE THINK THAT'S WHAT'S WRONG WITH THE FREEZE, REV.

WE'VE GOT TO START SOMEWHERE, MIKE.

WELL? WHAT DO YOU THINK?

I THINK IT'S THE MOST PROVOCATIVE NUCLEAR NEWS-LETTER I'VE EVER READ!

YOU DO? REALLY?

ABSOLUTELY. YOUR PASTORAL LETTER ON DETERRENCE SEEMS WELL-REASONED AND RIGHT ON TARGET..

ALSO, THE PHONE INTERVIEW WITH ARCHBISHOP BERNAR-DIN WAS WELL HANDLED, AS WAS THE NUCLEAR ROUND-UP COLUMN. I EVEN LIKED THE HOROSCOPE!

WELL, THAT'S JUST A CIRCULATION BOOST-ER.

"LEO: EXERCISE DIPLOMACY TODAY. TRY TO AVOID SHOWDOWNS."

SO WHAT'S THE RESPONSE TO YOUR NEWS-LETTER BEEN LIKE SO FAR, REV?

MOSTLY POSITIVE, MIKE. IT'S BEEN VERY GRATIFYING.

THINK IT WILL HAVE SOME IMPACT?

WELL, I THINK ANYTHING THAT CONTRIBUTES TO THE DIALOGUE ABOUT NUCLEAR MO-RALITY HELPS..

ESPECIALLY ON A DECISION-MAKING LEVEL. THAT'S WHY I SENT COPIES OF MY PEACE MESSAGE TO A FEW PLACES WHERE IT COULD MAKE A DIFFERENCE!

ANOTHER SOVIET NEWS-LETTER JUST CAME IN, SIR.

GOSH, DON'T THOSE PEOPLE EVEN LET UP FOR CHRISTMAS?

WHAT ARE YOU DO-ING, JOANIE? WE'RE SUPPOSED TO BE PRACTICING PANT-ING..

I CAN'T. >GASP!< I'M HAVING CONTRAC-TIONS AGAIN.

CONTRACTIONS? YOU'RE STILL HAVING CON-TRACTIONS?

YEAH. EVERY FEW MINUTES. WHAT DO YOU THINK WE SHOULD DO?

UM.. I DON'T KNOW. I MEAN, YOU'RE NOT DUE FOR TWO WEEKS.

SO?

SO WE STILL HAVE ONE MORE CLASS. I'M NOT FULLY TRAINED!

>PUFF!< SO RAISE YOUR HAND AND ASK!

WHAT SORT OF PAIN, ABDOMINAL?

YES, AND THE.. >GASP!< THE.. CONTRACTIONS ARE EVERY TWO TO FIVE MINUTES..

HMM.. IT'S PROBABLY JUST FALSE LABOR..

PROBABLY.. >PUFF! PUFF!< CHECK THE BOOK.. THE CONTRACTIONS ARE LASTING ABOUT 60 SECONDS.. UHN!

OKAY, LET'S SEE.. CONTRACTIONS ARE EVERY TWO TO FIVE MINUTES, LASTING FOR..

>PUFF!<

OH, MY GOD! YOU'RE HAVING A BABY!

I AM? WHAT'S IT SAY?

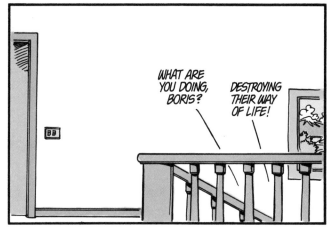

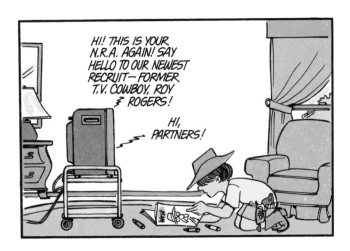

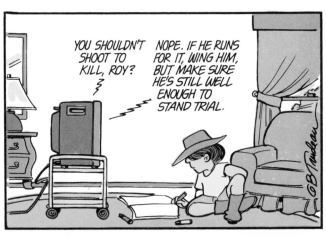

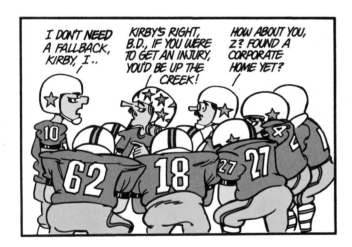

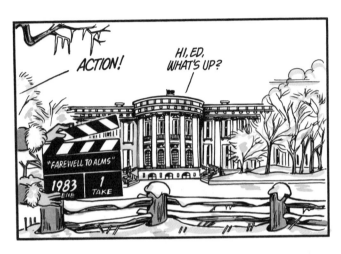

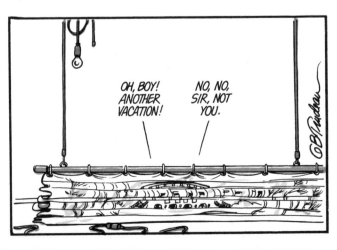